biblical GARDEN COOkERY

eileen GADEN

Christian Herald Books
40 Overlook Drive, Chappaqua, New York 10514

DEDICATION

To Allan without whose encouragement and assistance this book would not have been written.

PREFACE

I find a special pleasure in traveling in the Holy Land and in learning about its history and people. In this place where the old and the new exist side by side, biblical scenes are glimpsed at every turn. Among the poor, native, country people of the Middle East, foods and cooking methods have changed little after thousands of years. A Sarah may be seen baking her daily bread; a Rebekah may be cooking a fragrant stew; a group of women may join in preparing festive feasts celebrated today as in biblical times.

From these peoples and from careful reading of rich scriptural sources, we have a good understanding about food and its preparation in biblical times. Although no recipes as such have come down to us, we do know which foods were in use. The return to foods naturally grown, home gardening, and the enhancing of simple, wholesome, delicious meals with herbs and spices—this too is a part of the rich heritage we reap from the Bible. We are moving full circle to reach again the ancient wisdom from Ecclesiastes 1:9: "the thing that hath been, it is that which shall be; and that which is done is that which shall be done; and there is no new thing under the sun."

Our modern foods are similar to those recorded in the Bible and improved descendants of them. Some foods were not known to biblical people, such as tomatoes, green peppers, corn, and citrus fruit. But their foods did not lack variety and interest. Indeed, their use of nuts, vegetables, fish, fruit, cheeses, and the natural sweetener, honey, undoubtedly contributed to long and productive lives.

Much research has gone into making this book as authentic as possible in the ingredients included. Only foods mentioned in the Bible or documented in Jewish writings of the time have been used. Substitutions for various foods are given, though the flavor of the end result will differ.

Our methods of cooking have changed with the advent of the blender, the electric beater, and controlled ovens. However, food can still be made according to ancient methods, and the recipes in this book need only a bowl, a whisk, a cutting board, knife, fork, spoon, and a few pans. In biblical times with no refrigeration, everything was prepared and consumed each day. Meat became tender by hanging or marinating; milk was drunk on the sour side and herbs and spices were pungent enough to hide any suspected spoilage.

A new recipe format is used in this book for convenience and clarity. All ingredients are listed in large type in the left column and the quantities needed appear in the right column.

A few ingredients may be difficult to find, but they are worth searching out. Find the pomegranate juice (which many prefer to cranberry juice), or the carob powder (a fine substitute for those who have problems with eating chocolate) in health food stores or by mail order. Excellent goat and ewe cheeses are available from many countries. Roquefort and Gorgonzola from Italy are sheep cheeses, as is the Greek Feta. Capricette and Chevre are goat cheeses from France.

A special attribute of many recipes in this book is the combination of herbs and spices from biblical times. Because fresh and home-grown herbs are so much better than those found in the store and because herb gardening demands so little time and space, a final section of this book gives information on herb gardening and herbs. A windowsill or tiny plot is all that is needed for a pest-free, useful, and fragrant garden.

A delightful addition to the book are the drawings by the talented artist Ted Handke, who has captured the tranquility and the antiquity of the land.

Eileen Gaden.

INTRODUCTION

And God said, "Behold, I have given you every herb bearing seed . . . and every tree . . ."
GENESIS 1:29

Eve's temptation; Esau selling his birthright for a bowl of lentil pottage; Moses calling forth manna from heaven; Christ feeding thousands with five loaves of bread and two fishes—these are Bible scenes familiar to us all from childhood.

A history of prophets, patriarchs and kings, the Bible is also a drama woven from the lives of farmers, shepherds and homemakers —all absorbed, as we are today, in earning daily bread, raising families, and enjoying the fruits of their labors.

Food was important to every aspect of life in ancient times: religion, art, trade, and government. Cattle and crops were the main forms of wealth. Even the biblical unit of measurement, the cubit, was arrived at by placing grains of barley end to end. Of the two hundred occupations mentioned in the Bible, almost a quarter of them are related to the growing, trading, and preparing of food. Bakers, banquet managers, and spice merchants did a brisk business in the crooked streets and flat-roofed homes of old Jerusalem. Many of the miracles, proverbs, and parables of the Bible begin with food and daily events in a farming society.

Most of the events recorded in the Bible took place in an area no larger than Vermont. Once known as Palestine, this "fertile crescent" of land nestled between the huge empires of Egypt and Mesopotamia. On a clear day, one naturalist has noted, a sharp-eyed eagle in flight could see this entire area from end to end. Yet the birthplace of the Bible is a world-in-small. A kaleidoscope of contrasts in landscape, climate, plant and animal life, the Holy Land shifts abruptly from oases shaded by date palms to highlands; from Mount Sinai where Moses saw the burning bush to the Jordan Valley Rift, the lowest point on earth; from the desert where Jesus fasted for forty days to the Sea of Galilee where Peter's nets teemed with fish.

And the climate is as varied as the landscape, with seasons of snow and desert heat, floods and droughts, hail and wind storms. While the peak of Mount Hermon glistens with snow, a hundred miles away tropical breezes blow along the shores of the Dead Sea; while fruit is ripening in Jericho, there may be hail in Jerusalem!

Crossroads of the ancient world, where the main trade routes of Europe, Africa and Asia intersect, the Holy Land was also the meeting ground of an almost endless variety of plants and animals. Of the more than two thousand different trees and plants and over seven hundred species of mammals in the area today, many were first described in the pages of the Old and New Testaments. With this wide range of environments, it's small wonder that our biblical forefathers cultivated and enjoyed many of the fruits, vegetables, fish and meat we find in our own gardens and markets today. Barley, wheat, lentils and millet for bread, grapes, nuts, olives, and seeds from which oil was pressed—these were staple crops sewn long before Christ's birth.

The simple people cooked meals either in open courtyards or indoors; they ate from one large communal earthenware dish while sitting on mats or skins. Women of the family were busy before dawn, grinding barley and wheat into meal, baking the day's first flat bread on hot stones, milking goats and ewes.

It was customary to have only two meals a day. The farmer in the field and the city dweller started the day with a morning morsel of a few olives or nuts before work began. At noon, resting from the heat of midday, families ate meals consisting of bread soaked in vinegar with some parched corn (Ruth 2:14), or pottage and bread, or bread and fish (John 21:9). Dinner, the principal meal of the day

INTRODUCTION

was eaten just before or after sunset. This repast could have started with an appetizer of cucumbers, radishes and cheese accompanied by the ever present bread and some refreshing drink. Usually fish, vegetables or perhaps some lamb followed. For dessert, sweetmeats made with figs, dates and honey with a choice of melon, apricot or pomegranate rounded out the leisurely meal.

If everyday fare was meager, there were also times and places of feasting. Certainly the kings of the Bible dined well and entertained on a grand scale. The earliest recorded menu describes an Egyptian banquet, held almost a thousand years before Christ's birth, which lasted ten days and nights and was attended by more than seventy thousand people! At one of King Solomon's banquets, the golden tables would have been laden with dishes to delight even the most distinguished palates. After wandering through his lavish palace or his famed gardens, fragrant with olive and almond trees and spices and graced by brilliant peacocks, we would have dined on beef, mutton, fish, imported delicacies, and rich pastries. At the court of Herod, we would have dined more sumptuously still, in Roman style, with exotic appetizers of squid and conch, and a main course of flaming tongues or wild boar.

The feasts of most of our biblical forefathers, though more modest, were celebrated with equal gusto and evolved originally in rhythm with the farmer's seasons. The three earliest festivals we know of were held during the harvests of barley, wheat and summer fruit. The first, a spring festival which later became the Passover, began as a double celebration of lambing and the barley harvest. The Feast of Weeks was a summer feast enjoyed at the beginning of the wheat harvest. The third, known as the Feast of the In-gathering, was much like our own New Year's holiday. It was celebrated in autumn with dancing, grape-harvesting, food-making, and days of feasting and song. It was on these special occasions that the meat of lambs and goats was offered in worship as thanksgiving for abundant harvests. Whether a simple meal or a feast, eating in biblical times was always accompanied by thanksgiving.

biblical garden cookery

OFFERINGS
appetizers   1

IN THE BEGINNING
soups   13

FROM THE GARDEN OF EDEN
fruits and nuts   25

GREENS OF THE EARTH
vegetables and salads   44

MANNA FROM HEAVEN
breads and grains   69

THE LAND OF MILK AND HONEY
cheeses, yogurts, buttermilk, desserts   95

FISH OF THE SEA
haddock, sole, salmon, cod, bass   116

SEA CREATURES WITH SHELLS
shrimp, clams, oysters, scallops, lobsters   125

CONTENTS

BIRDS OF THE AIR
duck, goose, dove, partridge, quail   132

BIRDS OF THE COURTYARD
chicken and eggs   140

ANIMALS OF THE HILLS
lamb, goat, pork   148

ANIMALS OF THE PASTURELAND
beef and veal   161

HUNTER'S REWARD
kidneys, hearts, liver, tongue, sweetbreads, brains   172

ODDMENTS
stuffings, sauces, dressings   178

FOR THOSE WHO THIRST
beverages   186

SOME BIBLICAL GARDENS
herb gardening   190

index   204

OFFERINGS

Speak unto the children of Israel, that they bring me an offering . . .

EXODUS 25:2

Travelers and arriving guests were immediately offered olives, fruits, salt fish, or bread. This age-old custom has lasted and today we too offer our friends similar tokens of hospitality.

ROQUEFORT COINS

ROQUEFORT CHEESE	1/4 pound, crumbled
BUTTER	1/4 pound, soft
CREAM	2 tablespoons, heavy
EGG YOLK	1
UNBLEACHED FLOUR	or all-purpose, 1 1/3 cups
MUSTARD	1/4 teaspoon, dry
EGG WHITE	1, slightly beaten with 1 tablespoon water

Cream ROQUEFORT CHEESE and BUTTER together and mix in heavy CREAM and EGG YOLK. Stir in FLOUR and MUSTARD and mix well. Form into a ball; wrap and chill until firm. Roll dough on a lightly floured board to 1/8 inch thickness; cut into 1 1/2 inch rounds with floured cutter. Place on an ungreased baking sheet and brush with beaten EGG WHITE. Bake in a preheated 425°F. oven until lightly browned and puffed, about 6 minutes. Makes about 7 dozen coins.

CHEESE AND ANCHOVY SPREAD

ROQUEFORT CHEESE	6 ounces, crumbled
CREAM CHEESE	1/2 cup, at room temperature
ANCHOVY FILLETS	3, chopped and mashed
EGGS	3, hard-cooked, finely chopped
PARSLEY	1/4 cup, finely chopped
FENNEL BULBS	1 or 2, sliced, or celery stalks

Cream the 2 CHEESES together; work in the ANCHOVY FILLETS and add the EGGS and PARSLEY. Place in a mound in the center of a platter and surround with FENNEL slices. Makes about 1 1/4 cups.

WATERCRESS SPREAD

CAPRICETTE	or cream cheese, 8 ounces
MILK	2 tablespoons
WATERCRESS	1/4 cup, finely chopped
SALT	
PEPPER	

Mix together CHEESE, MILK and WATERCRESS with SALT and PEPPER to taste. Bring to room temperature before serving. Spread on dark bread. Makes about 1 1/4 cups.

RADISH CHEESE SPREAD

CHEVRE	or cream cheese, 4 ounces
SOUR CREAM	1/2 cup
RADISHES	2 tablespoons, finely minced
PARSLEY	2 tablespoons, finely chopped
FENNEL SEED	freshly ground, 1/2 teaspoon
SALT	

Mix the CHEESE and SOUR CREAM together; add RADISHES, PARSLEY and FENNEL. Add SALT to taste. Serve with dark bread for an appetizer. Makes about 1 1/4 cups.

FRIED CHEESE

PIORA CHEESE	or Gruyere or Munster, 1 pound
FLOUR	5 tablespoons
EGGS	3, large, slightly beaten
BREAD CRUMBS	dry, 1 1/2 cups
OIL	

Slice CHEESE 1/2 inch by 1/2 inch thick and 2 inches long. Dredge with FLOUR then dip into beaten EGGS and BREAD CRUMBS two times. Fry in 2 inches of OIL, 380°F. on frying thermometer, until golden. Remove with slotted spoon and drain on paper towel. Fry only 4 or 5 at a time in a small pan; they cook almost instantly.

BLACK OLIVE AND CHEESE SAVORY

CHABICHOU CHEESE	or cream cheese, 4 ounces, at room temperature
BRYNDZA CHEESE	or Roquefort, 1/4 cup, crumbled
BLACK OLIVES	preferably Calamata, 2 tablespoons, pitted and chopped
FENNEL BULB	or celery, 1/4 cup, chopped
ONION	2 tablespoons, finely chopped
CREAM	heavy

Cream the CHEESES together. Mix in the next 3 ingredients with enough CREAM to make spreadable. Makes about 1 cup.

SHEPHERD'S SPREAD

ROQUEFORT CHEESE	4 ounces
CAPRICETTE	or cream cheese, 8 ounces
SAGE	fresh, chopped, 2 teaspoons or dried to taste
ONION JUICE	2 teaspoons

Thoroughly cream the two cheeses together and blend in the SAGE and ONION JUICE. Bring to room temperature before serving. Makes about 1 cup.

POTTED TONGUE

TONGUE	beef, smoked, cooked, 1/2 pound
BUTTER	3/4 cup
MACE	ground, 1/4 teaspoon
SALT	
PEPPER	

Mash TONGUE to a paste or put in a blender. Cream together the TONGUE, BUTTER and MACE; add SALT and PEPPER to taste. Fill crocks or jars with tight fitting lids with the mixture and refrigerate. Will keep several weeks under refrigeration. Makes about 1 3/4 cups.

CUCUMBERS WITH WALNUT DRESSING

GARLIC	2 cloves
WALNUTS	6 tablespoons, chopped
SALT	3/4 teaspoon
VINEGAR	1 1/2 tablespoons
OLIVE OIL	6 tablespoons
CUCUMBER	1 large, peeled and chopped
ENDIVES	4

Pound the GARLIC, WALNUTS and SALT together in a mortar and pestle or grind in a blender. Gradually add the VINEGAR and OIL. Pour over the CUCUMBER; chill. Serve in a bowl surrounded by ENDIVE leaves. Serves 4 as an appetizer.

HEBRON CHICKEN LIVER AND EGG SPREAD

GARLIC	1 clove, minced
CHICKEN LIVERS	1/2 pound
BUTTER	1 tablespoon

EGGS	2, hard-cooked, chopped
ONION JUICE	2 teaspoons
MUSTARD SEED	1/4 teaspoon, ground
ANISE SEED	1/2 teaspoon, ground
SOUR CREAM	1/4 cup
JAVAN DRESSING	p. 185, 2 tablespoons
PARSLEY	1 tablespoon
SALT	
PEPPER	

Cook GARLIC and CHICKEN LIVERS in BUTTER; cool and chop. Combine LIVER mixture with EGGS and the remaining ingredients. Add SALT and PEPPER to taste. Mix thoroughly; chill. Serve with dark bread. Makes about 2 cups.

ESTHER'S APPETIZERS

Fold-Overs With Onion Or Meat Filling

PASTRY

UNBLEACHED FLOUR	or all-purpose, 2 cups
SALT	1 teaspoon
CURRY POWDER	1 1/2 teaspoons
BUTTER	3/4 cup
WATER	about 6 tablespoons
EGG	1, slightly beaten

Combine the first 3 ingredients in a bowl; cut in BUTTER until the mixture resembles coarse meal. Sprinkle with WATER and mix with a fork until all the FLOUR is moistened. Gather the dough together and press it firmly into a ball. Divide dough and roll to 1/8 inch thickness; cut with a 3 1/4 inch cookie cutter. Place 1 teaspoon of filling on one half of circle, fold over and seal edges by pressing together with a moistened fork. Brush with beaten EGG and bake in a preheated 375°F. oven for 8 to 10 minutes. Makes about 24 appetizers.

ONION FILLING

ONIONS 2 cups, finely chopped
OIL 1/4 cup

Cook ONIONS in OIL until golden. Drain on paper towel and sprinkle lightly with salt.

MEAT FILLING

PINE NUTS 1/4 cup
BUTTER 2 tablespoons
ONION 1/2 cup, finely chopped
BEEF 1/2 pound, ground
SALT
PEPPER

Cook PINE NUTS in BUTTER until lightly brown; remove. Add ONIONS and cook until tender. Stir in BEEF and cook until the pink disappears. Mix in the PINE NUTS and SALT and PEPPER to taste.

FRUIT FRITTERS

APRICOT JUICE 2 cups
FLOUR 2 cups
SALT 2 teaspoons
APRICOTS 1/2 pound, dried
DATES 1/2 pound
ALMONDS whole, toasted
OIL for frying

Mix JUICE, FLOUR and SALT together and blend until smooth. If APRICOTS are dry, simmer until soft but not mushy; drain and pat dry. Place an ALMOND in each pitted DATE and wrap in APRICOT; secure with a wooden pick. Dip into the JUICE batter and fry in OIL just long enough to become golden. Drain on paper. Serve hot from a covered dish.

BROILED FRESH FIGS AND DATES

BACON	about 9 slices
FIGS	fresh, black or green, 12
DATES	12
ROQUEFORT CHEESE	
CREAM CHEESE	
HAM	

Cut BACON into pieces long enough to wrap one time around the FIGS and DATES. Remove hard stem end of FIGS and cut a gash in the side. Mix together equal quantities of ROQUEFORT and CREAM CHEESE and fill the

FIGS; wrap in BACON, securing with a wooden pick. Pit the DATES and fill with equal quantities of CREAM CHEESE and HAM; wrap in BACON. Thread the FIGS and DATES on a long skewer and broil, turning several times, until the BACON is crisp. Serve hot from the skewer or keep hot in a small covered dish.

STUFFED GRAPE LEAVES

BULGUR	uncooked or rice, 1/2 cup
ONION	1 small, finely chopped
PARSLEY	1/4 cup, finely chopped
MINT LEAVES	1/4 cup, finely chopped
EGG	1, beaten
PEPPER	1/8 teaspoon, freshly ground
SALT	1 3/4 teaspoons
LAMB	1 pound, ground
***GRAPE LEAVES**	48, fresh or bottled, or romaine leaves
STOCK	beef or chicken, 2 cups
BUTTER	2 tablespoons

7

Combine and mix the first 6 ingredients with 3/4 teaspoon SALT; add LAMB and mix well. Place a rounded teaspoon of mixture in the center of each GRAPE LEAF; fold in sides and roll up. Place in a 3 quart saucepan, side by side and in layers. Add STOCK, BUTTER and remaining 1 teaspoon SALT. Put a heat proof plate inside the saucepan with a weight on it to press the GRAPE LEAVES down. Cover and simmer for 45 minutes. Drain stuffed leaves, reserving 1 cup STOCK. Place leaves on a serving dish and keep warm. Thicken the liquid with a little flour, if desired, and pour it over the leaves. Serve as appetizers.

PREPARATION OF GRAPE LEAVES

Fresh grape leaves should be stacked in a kettle and boiling water poured over. Boil for 1 minute with 1/2 teaspoon salt; leaves will turn olive green. Drain.

Bottled leaves should be drained and soaked in cold water for 15 minutes to remove salt. Boil for 1 minute with fresh water before using. Drain.

FLAVORED BUTTERS

WALNUT BUTTER

WALNUTS	3/4 cup, finely chopped
FENNEL BULBS	or celery, 1/2 cup, finely chopped
SALT	1/4 teaspoon
BUTTER	1/2 cup, soft

Combine and mix all ingredients together. Makes about 1 3/4 cups.

WATERCRESS BUTTER

WATERCRESS	1 cup, finely chopped
BUTTER	1/2 cup, soft
SALT	

Combine and mix WATERCRESS and BUTTER together; add SALT to taste. Makes about 3/4 cup.

EUPHRATES PICKLED HERRING

SALT HERRING	6
WATER	
ONIONS	2 medium, thinly sliced
VINEGAR	tarragon, 1 1/2 cup
SUGAR	3/4 cup
PEPPERCORNS	12
BAY LEAVES	4, small

Soak HERRING in cold WATER for 24 hours, changing the WATER several times. Drain and wipe dry. Split the HERRING into halves and bone it; cut into 1 inch size pieces. Place in a bowl with alternate layers of sliced ONIONS. Bring the VINEGAR to a boil and add remaining ingredients; pour over the HERRING. Let mixture cool; cover and refrigerate for 2 days before serving. Serve as an appetizer.

STUFFED EGGS CYRENE

EGGS	12, hard-cooked, cut in half lengthwise
CAPERS	1 tablespoon, chopped
CHEVRE CHEESE	or cream cheese, 6 tablespoons
ERECH DRESSING	p. 182, or French dressing
SALT	
PEPPER	
DILL SAUCE	p. 10
RADISHES	3 or 4
PARSLEY	12 sprigs

Remove the yolks from the whites and press through a sieve. Mix yolks with CAPERS and CHEESE. Moisten with ERECH DRESSING and SALT and PEPPER to taste. Fill whites with yolk mixture and press 2 halves together. Arrange EGGS on a serving dish and coat each with DILL

SAUCE. Garnish with RADISHES and PARSLEY. Makes 12 appetizers.

DILL SAUCE

JAVAN DRESSING	p. 183, or mayonnaise, 3/4 cup
ONION JUICE	1 tablespoon
LIQUID FROM CAPERS	2 tablespoons
DILL	fresh, chopped, 1 teaspoon or 1/2 teaspoon dried
SALT	
PEPPER	

Combine the first 4 ingredients and mix well. SALT and PEPPER to taste.

TENDER THISTLES
Stuffed Artichoke Leaves

ARTICHOKES	4, cooked, chilled
EGGS	2 hard-cooked, finely chopped
CAPERS	small, 2 tablespoons
CHEESE	Chevre, Capricette or cream cheese, 2 tablespoons
JAVAN DRESSING	p. 183, or mayonnaise
SALT	
PEPPER	freshly ground white
PARSLEY	finely chopped

Remove the leaves and chokes from 4 cooked ARTI-CHOKES. Select the largest and best leaves and reserve. Mash the bottoms and mix with the chopped EGGS, CA-PERS and CREAM CHEESE. Moisten with JAVAN DRESSING. SALT and PEPPER to taste; chill. Cut off each reserved leaf squarely, about 2 inches from the base. Spoon some of the chilled mixture onto the base of each leaf and sprinkle with chopped PARSLEY. Place the filled leaves on a large round platter in concentric circles. Serve as an appetizer.

OFFERINGS

BULGUR AND MINT SALAD

BULGUR	1 cup, uncooked
WATER	
GREEN ONIONS	1 1/2 cups, finely chopped
PARSLEY	1 cup, finely chopped
MINT	fresh, 1/2 cup, finely chopped
OLIVE OIL	6 tablespoons
SALT	
PEPPER	
VINEGAR	2 to 4 tablespoons
ROMAINE LETTUCE	1 head, leaves separated

Wash BULGUR in cold water and drain. Pour over WA-
TER to cover and let soak 1 hour; drain well. Add the
ONIONS and crush ONIONS and BULGUR together with
finger tips. Add PARSLEY, MINT and OLIVE OIL; mix
well. SALT and PEPPER to taste. Add enough VINEGAR
to make it tart. Arrange BULGUR SALAD in the center of
a platter and surround with ROMAINE leaves. Scoop up
the SALAD with torn pieces of ROMAINE. Serves 6 as an
appetizer.

CILICIA CUCUMBERS

Salmon Salad Filling

CUCUMBERS	2 large
SALT	
SALMON	fresh cooked, 8 ounces
RADISHES	6 tablespoons, chopped
GREEN ONIONS	2 tablespoons, chopped
CAPERS	2 tablespoons
JAVAN DRESSING	p. 183
PARSLEY	16 small sprigs

Peel CUCUMBERS, slice in half and cut into 4 equal pieces;
remove enough seeds to form cups. Blot dry with a paper
towel. Lightly sprinkle with SALT. Flake SALMON and add
the next 3 ingredients; toss with JAVAN DRESSING to
moisten. When ready to serve, fill each section with the

salad and garnish with a sprig of PARSLEY. Canned salmon or tuna may be substituted. Makes 16 appetizers. Note: This may be used as luncheon dish if cucumbers are cut lengthwise in half and stuffed.

MINTED LAMB NUGGETS

LAMB	1 pound, ground
GARLIC	1 teaspoon, finely chopped
EGGS	2, lightly beaten
BREAD CRUMBS	1 cup stale
MINT	2 tablespoons chopped fresh or 1 tablespoon dried, crumbled
CINNAMON	1 teaspoon, ground
SALT	1 teaspoon
BUTTER	1/2 cup

Combine all ingredients except BUTTER in a bowl and mix well. Let stand 15 minutes; shape into 1 inch balls. Fry in BUTTER 3 to 5 minutes depending on desired doneness. Shake the pan continually to keep the nuggets round and evenly browned. Makes about 50 nuggets. Serve with Curried Javan Dressing (p. 176). Serves 12 as an appetizer.

SEABOBS

LOBSTER	1 1/4 pounds, cleaned, cooked
SHRIMP	medium, 1/2 pound, cleaned, cooked
SEA SCALLOPS	1/2 pound, poached 3 minutes

Cut the LOBSTER, SHRIMP and SCALLOPS into bite size pieces. Thread one of each onto a wooden pick. Makes about 40 seabobs. Serve with PARSLEY SAUCE (p. 183).

iN The BeGiNNiNG

In the beginning was the Word . . .
JOHN 1:1

A fine beginning for any meal is a delicious soup. Or a hearty soup, such as ill-fated Esau's lentil pottage, can be the center of a satisfying and nourishing meal. In biblical times, and often accompanied by barley bread, the broth was eaten first, followed by meat and vegetables from the cooking pot.

CREAM OF ALMOND SOUP ADORAIM

ALMONDS	1 cup, blanched, toasted and ground
ONION	1 medium, peeled and cut into quarters
CLOVES	2 whole
STOCK	chicken, 3 cups
BUTTER	2 tablespoons
FLOUR	2 tablespoons
MILK	1 cup
CREAM	heavy, 1 cup
SALT	

Put the first 4 ingredients in a medium saucepan; cover and simmer for 30 minutes. Discard the ONION and CLOVES; puree the ALMONDS and stock in blender. Melt the BUT-

TER in a 1 1/2 quart saucepan, add the FLOUR and cook 1 minute. Gradually add the MILK and cook until thickened. Stir the ALMOND puree into the thickened MILK; add CREAM and cook over low heat until hot. Add SALT to taste. Sprinkle with slivered, toasted ALMONDS. One or two drops of ALMOND EXTRACT may be added. Serves 4 to 6.

CREAM OF WATERCRESS DOTHAN

WATERCRESS	2 cups, finely chopped leaves and stems
ONION	4 thin slices, finely chopped
MILK	1 quart
EGG	1, slightly beaten
CREAM	heavy, 1/2 cup
NUTMEG	freshly grated, 1/4 teaspoon
SALT	
PEPPER	

In a medium saucepan, scald MILK with ONIONS; add WATERCRESS and gently simmer 15 minutes. Stir a little of the hot MILK mixture into beaten EGG and return to saucepan, stirring constantly. Add CREAM and NUTMEG. Reheat carefully without letting the soup boil; SALT and PEPPER to taste. Puree in blender if desired. Serves 6.

ROQUEFORT SOUP

STOCK	chicken, 3 1/2 cups
CREAM	medium, 1/2 cup
FLOUR	3 tablespoons
ROQUEFORT CHEESE	3 to 4 tablespoons, grated
PARSLEY	flat leaf, chopped, 1 tablespoon

Heat STOCK and CREAM. Mix FLOUR with some of the hot mixture to make a smooth paste and blend in with a whisk. Cook, over low heat, until thickened. Stir in the ROQUEFORT CHEESE and sprinkle with PARSLEY. Makes about 1 quart.

in the beginning

SPRING SOUP

SHALLOTS	3, finely chopped
BUTTER	2 tablespoons
WATERCRESS	1 cup, chopped
FLOUR	3 tablespoons
MILK	1 quart
SALT	
PEPPER	freshly ground, white

Cook SHALLOTS for 5 minutes in BUTTER; add WATERCRESS and cook 3 minutes more. Add FLOUR and slowly stir in the MILK; blend well and cook until thickened. Add SALT and PEPPER to taste. Puree in blender if desired. Makes about 1 quart.

PERSIAN CUCUMBER AND YOGURT SOUP

YOGURT	1 quart
BUTTERMILK	or milk, 1 cup
MINT	fresh, finely chopped, 1/2 cup or chopped green onions
CUCUMBERS	3 small, peeled, seeded and chopped
SALT	
PEPPER	freshly ground white
WALNUTS	1/2 cup, chopped

Beat the YOGURT and BUTTERMILK together until well blended. Stir in MINT and CUCUMBERS; SALT and PEPPER to taste. Serve very cold in individual bowls and sprinkle with chopped WALNUTS. Serves 8.

MILK AND HONEY SOUP

EGG YOLKS	2
HONEY	3 tablespoons
BUTTERMILK	1 quart
CREAM	heavy, 1/2 cup, whipped
ALMONDS	toasted, slivered, 1/4 cup

Beat EGG YOLKS until thick and lemon colored. Beat in

HONEY 1 tablespoon at a time. Stir in the BUTTERMILK and refrigerate. Serve in individual bowls with a dollop of WHIPPED CREAM. Garnish with ALMONDS. Serves 6.

KEDISH SUMMER SOUP

STOCK	chicken, 4 1/2 cups
DANDELION LEAVES	or sorrel, 1/2 cup, chopped
LETTUCE	chopped, 1 cup
WATERCRESS	1 cup, chopped
PARSLEY	1/4 cup, chopped
ONION	1 medium, chopped
SALT	1 1/4 teaspoons
PEPPER	freshly ground white, 1/4 teaspoon
CREAM	light, 3 cups
CHIVES	1 tablespoon, finely chopped

Bring the STOCK to a boil and drop in the greens, ONION, SALT and PEPPER. Cook 5 minutes, uncovered; puree. When ready to serve, add the CREAM and heat. Sprinkle with chopped CHIVES. Makes about 2 quarts.

BLACK OLIVE SOUP OF MAGDALA

STOCK	chicken, 4 cups
OLIVES	black, 1/2 cup, pitted, sliced, rinsed, preferably Greek Calamata
ONION JUICE	2 tablespoons
GARLIC	1 large clove, crushed
EGGS	2, beaten
CREAM	medium, 1 cup
SALT	
CORIANDER LEAVES	2 tablespoons, finely chopped

Combine STOCK and the next 3 ingredients in a saucepan. Simmer for 15 minutes; remove GARLIC. Mix beaten EGGS and CREAM together. Stir a few spoonfulls of the hot STOCK into the EGG mixture; beat well and return slowly to STOCK. Heat but do not boil; SALT to taste. Sprinkle with chopped CORIANDER. Serves 6.

OXTAIL SOUP

OIL	2 tablespoons
OXTAIL	2 pounds, cut into joints
BEEF	3/4 pound stew meat, cut into 1 1/2 inch pieces
ONIONS	2 large, sliced
FLOUR	1/4 cup, whole wheat or white
THYME	fresh, chopped, 1/2 teaspoon or 1/4 teaspoon dried
ROSEMARY	fresh, chopped, 1/2 teaspoon or 1/4 teaspoon dried
FENNEL SEED	crushed, 1/2 teaspoon
NUTMEG	freshly grated, 1/8 teaspoon
SALT	1 1/2 teaspoons
GARLIC	2 large cloves, chopped
WATER	3 quarts
BARLEY	1/4 cup
BAY LEAVES	2
PEPPER	freshly ground black

Heat OIL in a kettle and brown OXTAIL and BEEF. Remove and pour off all fat except 1 tablespoon. Brown the ONIONS and stir in FLOUR, herbs, spices, SALT and GARLIC; cook 1 minute stirring continually. Add the WATER slowly and stir until blended. Return OXTAIL and BEEF to kettle; add BARLEY and BAY LEAVES. Partially cover and simmer for 2 1/2 hours. Add freshly ground PEPPER and more SALT if necessary. Serves 6 to 8.

ONION SOUP SELEUCIA

BUTTER	1/2 cup
ONIONS	2 pounds, thinly sliced
STOCK	chicken, 4 cups
SALT	
PEPPER	freshly ground white

BREAD   6 slices, crusts removed, toasted and cut into 1/2 inch cubes

CHEESE   Romano or Parmesan, 4 ounces, grated

Cook ONIONS in BUTTER over low heat until tender but not brown. Add the CHICKEN STOCK and bring to a boil. Simmer 5 minutes; SALT and PEPPER to taste. Pour into a warm soup tureen over the toasted BREAD CUBES. Serve the grated CHEESE separately. Serves 4.

SCALLOP SOUP ALEXANDRIA

SHALLOTS	or green onions, chopped, 1/4 cup
GARLIC	1 large clove, finely chopped
BUTTER	1/4 cup
FLOUR	5 tablespoons
MILK	1 quart, scalded
SALT	1/2 teaspoon
PEPPER	white, freshly ground, 1/4 teaspoon
BAY LEAF	1, large
SCALLOPS	1 pound, cut into 1/2 inch pieces
PARSLEY	chopped, 2 tablespoons

Cook SHALLOTS and GARLIC in BUTTER until tender. Blend in FLOUR and cook 1 minute. Stir in MILK, SALT, and PEPPER; add BAY LEAF. Simmer 5 minutes. Drop in the SCALLOPS, return to a simmer and cook 5 minutes. Remove BAY LEAF and adjust the seasoning. Sprinkle with PARSLEY before serving. Serves 4.

BARLEY SOUP

BARLEY	1/2 cup, soaked overnight in water to cover
WATER	2 cups
SALT	1 teaspoon
BUTTER	3 tablespoons
ONION	1 cup, finely chopped
YOGURT	4 cups, plain
EGG	1, lightly beaten
FLOUR	1 tablespoon, unbleached
STOCK	chicken, 4 cups

PEPPER   freshly ground white
CORIANDER   2 tablespoons chopped fresh leaves or 1/2 tablespoon dried

Drain the BARLEY and place in a saucepan with 2 cups of WATER and SALT. Cover tightly and simmer until the BARLEY has absorbed all the liquid and grains are separated, about 1 hour. Add more WATER only if necessary. Cook ONION in BUTTER until soft but not brown. Stir in YOGURT. Remove from heat. Mix EGG and FLOUR together and blend into the YOGURT mixture. Bring the chicken STOCK to a boil in a large saucepan; stir in the YOGURT mixture and BARLEY. Add freshly ground PEPPER and SALT if needed. Pour into a warmed soup tureen and sprinkle with CORIANDER. Serves 8.

ESAU'S LENTIL POTTAGE

RED LENTILS	1 cup
BEEF STOCK	8 cups
OIL	1/4 cup
ONIONS	1 1/2 cups, coarsely chopped
FENNEL BULB	or celery, 1 cup, coarsely chopped
GARLIC	1 tablespoon, chopped
SAGE	fresh, chopped, 1 teaspoon or 1/2 teaspoon dried
SAVORY LEAVES	fresh, chopped, 1 teaspoon or 1/2 teaspoon dried
MUSTARD SEED	ground, 1/2 teaspoon or 1/4 teaspoon dry
SALT	1 teaspoon
PEPPER	freshly ground white, 1/4 teaspoon
PARSLEY	2 tablespoons, chopped

Wash LENTILS and boil for 2 minutes in BEEF STOCK. Remove from heat and skim if necessary. Cover and let stand 1 hour. Heat OIL and cook ONIONS, FENNEL and GARLIC until lightly colored; stir in herbs and MUSTARD SEED; reserve. Bring LENTILS to a boil again and simmer

1 hour. Stir in onion mixture. Cook 30 minutes more or until LENTILS are tender; correct seasoning. Sprinkle with chopped PARSLEY before serving. For a smooth soup put in blender. Makes about 2 quarts.

Note: Lamb broth or water and a ham bone may be substituted for stock.

CYPRUS LENTIL STEW

WATER	2 1/2 quarts
HAM HOCK	fresh or smoked, 1 pound
LENTILS	1 cup
ONIONS	3 large, quartered
GARLIC	3 large cloves, chopped
SALT	1 tablespoon
PEPPER	1/4 teaspoon, freshly ground
FENNEL BULB	or celery, 1 1/2 cups, coarsely chopped
MILLET	2 tablespoons
BARLEY	2 tablespoons
OREGANO	fresh, chopped, 1 teaspoon or 1/2 teaspoon dried
TARRAGON LEAVES	fresh, chopped, 1 teaspoon or 1/2 teaspoon dried

In a large kettle combine WATER and the next 6 ingredients. Partially cover and simmer 1 1/2 hours; stir occasionally from the bottom and skim when necessary. Add chopped FENNEL, MILLET, BARLEY and herbs and cook 1/2 hour longer. Remove meat from the bones and return the meat to the stew; pour into a warm soup tureen. Serve with a green salad. Serves 8.

PATMOS OYSTER STEW

MILK	2 cups
CREAM	light, 2 cups
OYSTERS	2 1/2 dozen
BUTTER	2 tablespoons
SALT	

PEPPER	freshly ground white
FENNEL	fresh leaves, chopped, 1/2 tablespoon
CORIANDER	fresh leaves, chopped, 1 tablespoon

Scald MILK and CREAM together. Put OYSTERS and their liquid into a saucepan with 2 tablespoons of BUTTER. Heat until OYSTERS plump and edges begin to curl. Add the OYSTERS and liquid to the MILK and CREAM. SALT and PEPPER to taste. Pour into a soup tureen and sprinkle with FENNEL and CORIANDER leaves. Serves 6.

PERGA CATCH

Mediterranean Fish Soup

STOCK	fish trimmings (bones, tails, and heads) plus 4 quarts of water or 2 quarts clam juice and 2 quarts water
ONION	1 medium, thinly sliced
GARLIC	2 large cloves, crushed
BAY LEAF	1 large
PEPPERCORNS	white and black, 1/4 teaspoon each
FENNEL SEED	ground, 1/2 teaspoon
VINEGAR	tarragon, 1 tablespoon
BUTTER	2 tablespoons
ONION	1 1/2 cups, finely chopped
EEL	1 1/2 pounds, skinned and cut crosswise into 1 inch pieces
PERCH	1 1/2 pounds, cleaned, trimmed and cut into 1 inch pieces
CARP	1 pound, cleaned, trimmed and cut into 1 inch pieces
DILL	fresh, chopped, 1 teaspoon or 1/2 teaspoon dried
THYME	fresh, chopped, 1 teaspoon or 1/2 teaspoon dried

21

SALT	
PEPPER	freshly ground white
PARSLEY	chopped, 2 tablespoons

Combine STOCK with the next 6 ingredients in a large kettle. Bring to a boil, reduce heat and simmer, partially covered, for 30 minutes. Strain STOCK into another container and discard fish trimmings and STOCK ingredients. Melt BUTTER in the kettle and cook the chopped ONIONS for 5 minutes. Add the fish, STOCK, DILL and THYME; cover and simmer 5 to 6 minutes or until fish flakes easily. Do not overcook. Add SALT and PEPPER to taste. Pour into a soup tureen and sprinkle with PARSLEY. Serves 8 to 10. Note: Four pounds of any variety of white fish may be substituted in this recipe.

CREAMY CHOWDER

BUTTER	1/4 cup
ONIONS	3 large, thinly sliced
FISH	2 pounds scrod or haddock fillets, cut into 1 1/2 inch pieces
FENNEL SEED	1/2 teaspoon, ground
BAY LEAVES	2
SALT	2 1/2 teaspoons
GARLIC	1 large clove, minced
WATER	2 1/2 cups
CREAM	light, 2 cups, scalded
PARSLEY	chopped

Cook ONIONS in BUTTER for 5 minutes; add the remaining ingredients except CREAM and PARSLEY. Bring to a boil, cover and simmer over low heat for 30 minutes. Add the hot CREAM. Serve in a tureen or casserole sprinkled with PARSLEY. Makes about 1 3/4 quarts.

BASIC BEEF STOCK

BONES	shinbones and knuckles, 1 1/2 pounds

iN the beGiNNiNG

BEEF	rump, 2 pounds, in one piece
WATER	4 quarts
SALT	1 teaspoon
PEPPERCORNS	8
BAY LEAF	1 large
ONIONS	2 medium, quartered, stuck with 2 cloves
PARSLEY	3 sprigs
CORIANDER LEAVES	or celery, chopped, 2 tablespoons
THYME	1 teaspoon, fresh, chopped, or 1/2 teaspoon dried
EGG WHITES	2
EGG SHELLS	2, crushed
COLD WATER	1/2 cup

Brown BONES and BEEF in a shallow open pan in a 450° oven. When well-browned, place them in a 6 quart kettle. Bring to a boil with WATER, skim, and add the next 7 ingredients. Simmer slowly, partially covered, for three hours, skimming from time to time. Discard BONES and remove BEEF (it may be thinly sliced and served cold with sauce). Do not add more salt to broth until ready to use in recipe. Strain broth through fine sieve or double thickness of damp cheesecloth. Chill; remove fat from top. Stock can be frozen in ice cube trays and stored in plastic bags for easy handling and future use. To clarify stock: beat EGG WHITES until stiff. Add them to the hot, strained stock. Drop the EGG SHELLS in and bring the mixture to a boil. Boil 2 minutes, then let stand 30 minutes; strain through damp flannel or double thickness of cheesecloth. Makes about 2 1/2 quarts of stock.

BASIC CHICKEN STOCK

CHICKEN	1 stewing or roasting
WATER	4 quarts
CORIANDER LEAVES	or celery, 3 teaspoons, coarsely chopped
LEEK	medium, 1 cut into 2 inch pieces, or 2 green onions

PARSLEY	3 sprigs
THYME	fresh, chopped, 1/2 teaspoon fresh or 1/4 teaspoon dried
MARJORAM	fresh, chopped, 1/2 teaspoon fresh or 1/4 teaspoon dried
BAY LEAF	1 large
SALT	1 teaspoon
PEPPERCORNS	6

Put CHICKEN in a large kettle and cover with the WATER. Bring to a boil and skim. Add the remaining ingredients. Partially cover and simmer slowly for 2 hours or until chicken is very tender. Remove the skin and bones and return them to the kettle to cook another hour. Save CHICKEN for future recipe. Strain stock through damp flannel or double thickness of cheesecloth. Chill stock. After stock has chilled, remove the fat. Do not add more salt to stock until ready to use in recipe. Stock can be frozen in ice cube trays and stored in plastic bags for easy handling and future use. Makes about 2 1/2 quarts of stock.

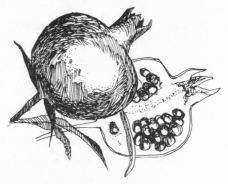

FROM THE GARDEN OF EDEN

*The Lord thy God bringeth thee into a good land
. . . a land of vines and fig trees and pomegranates.*
DEUTERONOMY 8:7, 8

*I made me gardens and orchards and I planted trees in
them of all kinds of fruit.* ECCLESIASTES 2:5

And a good land it was, rich with fruit and fragrant with the blossoms of the flowering trees. A land where grapes grew as large as plums, where golden apricots ripened and the juicy, pink-fleshed watermelon quenched many a summer thirst. A land of abundant figs, dates and pomegranates to sweeten the days of our forefathers, along with almonds, pistachios, and walnuts.

So important was fruit to mankind in Bible times that plucking an apricot or fig from a newly planted tree was forbidden by law. Only after the tree had grown untouched for five years could its fruits be gathered and enjoyed.

We have been told it was Eve's eating of the "forbidden fruit" that caused man's exile from Paradise. But just what was the fruit that Eve ate on that fatal day? Though never mentioned by name, it was a fruit of attractive appearance. Could it have been the quince, the apple, the ripening pomegranate, or the sweet apricot? Down through the ages, famous painters such as Michelangelo and Leonardo da Vinci have portrayed the Christ child holding various fruits. The apple, however, no longer bears the blame for the fall, because most scholars and botanists say that the soil and the climate were not suitable at that time, though apples flourish in Israel today.

The apricot seems to best answer the description and requirements of the forbidden fruit, and it is a likely choice as the most abundant fruit in the Holy Land except for the fig. Known as "golden apples," apricots were first brought to Palestine from Armenia in the time of Noah. In a land of sand and desert wind, the apricot was prized for its beautiful color, its sweet, refreshing fragrance, and delicate moistness. "A word fitly spoken is like apples of gold in pictures of silver," according to Proverbs 25:11. The Song of Solomon also sings the praises of this luscious fruit: "As the apple [apricot] tree among the trees of the wood, so is my beloved among the sons" (Song of Solomon 2:3). A legend tells of a room in Solomon's palace painted with murals showing apricot trees in full bloom. And so lovely and lifelike was their fruit that they seemed to breathe forth a sweet perfume as guests passed by.

The very first plant named in Genesis is the fig tree, for Adam and Eve covered themselves with its leaves. The fig is one of the most common fruits in Palestine. It is one of the few plants which still grows wild today.

Since the fig tree bears both a summer and a winter crop, there was never a shortage of the fruit. Its sweet taste was welcome to many a weary traveler, whether eaten fresh from the tree or dried and threaded on strings, pressed into cakes, or made into beverages. A basket of figs or fig cakes was often given as a present to an honored guest or visitor. When King David was traveling in the wilderness, Abigail, the wife of a local patriarch, hastened to greet him and took "an hundred clusters of raisins, and two hundred cakes of figs" (I Samuel 25:18).

Besides nourishing the body, the fig tree had other uses: its large leaves were fashioned into baskets, dishes, mats and umbrellas. The shade of a full grown fig tree is said to be cooler and more refreshing than that of an enclosed tent, which explains why it was favored for planting in biblical courtyards and gardens. Every Israelite longed for the peace and serenity pictured by the prophet Micah when he spoke of the coming of Christ:

> *They shall beat their swords into plowshares, and their spears into pruning hooks: nation shall not lift up a sword against nation, neither shall they learn war any more. But they shall sit every man under his vine and under his fig tree; and none shall make them afraid.*
>
> *Micah 4:3, 4*

Dates have been called the "food of the desert." So common were they in the Jordan Valley that Jericho was known as the "city of palm trees" (Deuteronomy 34:3). The date was the mainstay of the merchant caravans on their long, hot journeys; the palm tree a symbol of hope and survival for the desert wanderer. Since the tree grows only in oases or near springs, a weary traveler knew he would find not only fruit, but water.

Whatever other foods the multitudes lacked during famines and lean years, they probably always had dates, since the average palm produces about one hundred pounds of fruit every season and has a life span of sixty years or more. The palm has always been a symbol of life and fertility:

> *The righteous shall flourish like the palm tree . . . Those that be planted in the house of the Lord shall flourish . . . They shall bring forth fruit in old age.*
>
> *Psalms 92:12–14*

Cheaper than wheat and said to be more nutritious than barley, dates were a delicacy for peasants and kings. When pressed and exposed to the air, the pulp of the date turns into a thick syrup which was used in puddings, sweetmeats and pastries. This date juice was also an ingredient in spiced drinks. The Arabs have a saying that there are as many uses for dates as there are days in the year; Herodotus describes "bread . . . and honey as but a few of the fruits of the palm tree." Many believe that the honey mentioned in the Bible was in fact often the syrup of the date, for the honeybee is described only four times.

The pomegranate, whose name means "apple with seeds," was another desired fruit, although one which we seldom find in our markets today. Grown from antiquity and common now in Palestine, Egypt, and Syria, this sweet red fruit has a rich history. Its origin was in India, where it was cultivated by kings; it was grown in the fabulous Hanging Gardens of Babylon. The pomegranate was one of the rich samples the spies carried from "the land of milk and honey" (Numbers 13:23).

Since Solomon's time, the pulp of the pomegranate has not only been eaten raw, but squeezed to make fresh and cooling summer drinks; the roots of the tree and the rind were used in medicine. The first sherbet ever eaten was created from pomegranate juice mixed with mountain snow. The seeds were often dried, sprinkled with grenadine syrup, which was made from the fruit of the pomegranate, and eaten as a sweet. The large number of seeds found in each fruit makes it the symbol of fertility.

The beauty of the flower, leaves, and fruit are described many times in the Bible, especially in the lovely verses of the Song of Solomon:

> *Thy lips are like a thread of scarlet, and thy speech is comely; thy*
> *temples are like a piece of pomegranate within thy locks . . . Thy*
> *plants are an orchard of pomegranates, with pleasant fruits.*
> *The Song of Solomon 4:3, 13*

In art, too, the praises of the pomegranate were sung and designs of its delicate leaves and unusual globed fruit were carved by sculptors and embroidered in scarlet and blue on the borders of priestly robes. Even golden coins were etched to resemble the fruit, perhaps in the hope that the coins would multiply like pomegranate seeds!

The small, sturdy quince tree and the melon vine added richly to the fruits of the land. Native to northern Persia and Asia Minor, the quince was prized for its sweet fragrance, although the round, yellow-green fruit was tart rather than sweet to the taste. Not so the water-melon, which has been cultivated in Egypt and Palestine from pre-history. Along with the muskmelon, this fruit provided food, drink,

FROM the GARDEN OF EDEN

and medicine for rich and poor alike. Ripening all through the months of summer and fall, the melons were eaten fresh from the field, or the pulp was crushed and its juice mixed with honey for a thirst quencher which was once as popular as our lemonade is today. Even the seed of the fruit was roasted, salted and eaten, perhaps as an appetizer or a midday snack. The melon season was welcomed by the poor as the best harvest-time of the year; some of the fruit carried from the fields could weigh more than thirty pounds.

Most of the gardens referred to in the Bible were actually olive groves, with perhaps a few fig or nut trees and spice bushes to provide fruit, fragrance, and shade. It was most fitting that the dove of Noah signalled the end of the flood with the leaf of one of the world's oldest trees: "And the dove came in to him in the evening; and lo, in her mouth was an olive leaf plucked off" (Genesis 8:11). These ancient, hardy, gnarled, silvery trees were the only plants of any size to grow in some parts of the desert, where their beautiful white flowers bloomed in proud defiance of the sun and sand. It was under the many branched, twisted trunk of the olive tree that Christ spent his last night on earth in the Garden of Gethsemane, waiting and watching for the dawn.

One large olive tree was a priceless source of food and lumber and yielded half a ton of oil a year—more than enough to fill the cooking pots and light the lamps of an entire family. Harvest time for the olive crop came in October, at the end of the grape-picking season. The ripe olives were beaten from the trees with long poles and then gathered into woven baskets. Some fruit was always left on the highest branches:

> *When thou beatest thine olive tree, thou shalt not go over the boughs again; it shall be for the stranger, for the fatherless, and for the widow.*
>
> *Deuteronomy 24:20*

Once harvested, the oil was squeezed slowly from the fruit in an olive press, usually made of stone and wood, and stored in large vats. Olive oil was an important ingredient in bread and other foods. Even the poorest of families could make bread and offer a loaf in thanksgiving:

29

biblical garden cookery

The walnut tree was especially desired for its shady boughs, fragrant
leaves and delicious nutmeats. In the garden of Solomon at Etham,
a few miles from Jerusalem, the trees produced Persian walnuts.
Once fallen, the nutmeats were eaten from their shells, or baked into
bread and cakes; the walnut oil was used in cooking and soap making.

The pistachio tree grew wild and abundantly on the rocky hills of
Lebanon and Palestine. Pistachio kernels were eaten raw or fried with
salt and pepper. They were a popular dessert confection in the Orient; oil pressed from the kernels was used as a flavoring for sweets
and in cooking.

The word for almond in ancient Hebrew means "gift from God."
The almond tree is the first in the Holy Land to flower, beginning
in late winter. When the beautiful white blossoms with pink tinges
burst forth, it is a sign of winter's passing and the coming of spring.

Almonds were often eaten green before the shells hardened, and
the kernels were sometimes made into sweetmeats. Actually there are
two varieties of almond trees, the sweet or edible almond and the
bitter which is the source of almond flavoring. The bitter almond
contains a poisonous acid and must be processed before being used,
though a few of the kernels may l e added to a dish to impart the
elusive flavor without harm. The oil of the almond was important not
only in cooking, but also used in lotions, creams and powders for
thousands of years.

Fir trees are mentioned in Hosea 14:8: "I am like a green fir tree.
From me is thy fruit found." These were the nuts found in the layers
of the pine cones of the evergreen tree, a delectable treat eaten raw
or cooked with other foods. There were the only four edible nuts
indigenous to the Holy Land: the almond, pine, pistachio, and walnut.

Two very different trees which added variety were the citron and
the carob. The first was a small and beautiful tree thought to be the
"goodly tree" of Eden by some. Its fruit was the thick skinned citron
or etrog which was used as a ceremonial fruit in the Temple during

the Feast of the Tabernacles. The rind was often candied and eaten as a sweetmeat. The juice was milder, more fragrant, and sweeter to the taste than our lemon, which it resembles in appearance, though it is larger. Citrus fruits, including lemons, oranges, and limes, were unknown in Palestine and Egypt during Bible times.

Very common throughout the Holy Land was the handsome evergreen carob tree, sometimes called the "locust tree." This unusual flowering tree has six to eight inch pods. The pods, when ripe, are full of a dark, honey-like substance with the sweetness of manna and the flavor of chocolate. The ground pulp was made into sweet cakes and candy while the pods were given to the poor or used as cattle feed.

Although the biblical people lacked some of our fruits, they did have enough variety to make rich and varied desserts and preserves.

ABIGAIL'S APRICOT WHIP

APRICOTS	dried, 1 pound
WATER	2 1/2 cups
SALT	1/8 teaspoon
SUGAR	1/2 cup or to taste
ALMOND EXTRACT	1/2 teaspoon
CREAM	heavy, 1 1/2 cups

Cook APRICOTS in WATER and SALT until tender, about 20 minutes. Stir in the SUGAR and flavoring. Press through a sieve or puree in a blender; chill. Beat CREAM until stiff and fold into puree; chill. Serves 6.

FIG HERMITS

DRIED FIGS	1/2 pound
BUTTER	1/2 cup
SUGAR	3/4 cup
EGGS	2, unbeaten
HONEY	1/2 cup
UNBLEACHED FLOUR	or all-purpose, 2 3/4 cups
BAKING POWDER	3 teaspoons
SALT	1/2 teaspoon
FRUIT JUICE	2 tablespoons
WALNUTS	1/2 cup, chopped

Cover FIGS with cold water and simmer 10 minutes; drain and chop. Cream BUTTER and SUGAR together, add EGGS and HONEY and beat well. Mix dry ingredients together and add to the BUTTER-SUGAR mixture; stir in the FRUIT JUICE, FIGS and NUTS. Drop by teaspoonfuls 2 inches apart onto a greased cookie sheet. Bake in a preheated 375°F. oven for 6 to 8 minutes or until done. Cool slightly before removing from cookie sheet. Makes about 4 dozen.

SPICED DATE CHUTNEY

VINEGAR	tarragon, 1 3/4 cups
SUGAR	1 1/4 cups
WATER	1/4 cup
GARLIC	1 teaspoon, minced
DATES	2 cups (1 pound), pitted and coarsely chopped
GINGER	fresh, chopped, 1 teaspoon or 1/2 teaspoon dried
CORIANDER SEED	1/4 teaspoon, ground
MUSTARD SEED	1/4 teaspoon, ground
ANISE SEED	1/8 teaspoon, ground
CINNAMON	1/8 teaspoon, ground
SALT	1/4 teaspoon
PEPPER	white, 1/8 teaspoon, ground

Combine the first 4 ingredients in a saucepan and simmer 5 minutes. Add remaining ingredients and cook over low heat, stirring until just thickened, depending on dates, about 5 minutes. Spoon into hot sterilized jars and seal or store in a covered jar in refrigerator. Let mellow a week and serve with lamb or poultry. Makes about 2 half pint jars.

NINEVEH NUGGETS

BUTTER	1/3 cup
SUGAR	1/3 cup
HONEY	2/3 cup
EGG	1

ALMOND EXTRACT	1/4 teaspoon
FLOUR	2 2/3 cups
BAKING SODA	1 teaspoon
SALT	3/4 teaspoon
WALNUTS	chopped

Cream BUTTER and SUGAR; beat in HONEY and mix well. Stir in EGG and ALMOND EXTRACT. Sift together the FLOUR, BAKING SODA and SALT; add by fourths to the batter, beating well after each addition. Chill, form into 1 inch balls and roll in chopped WALNUTS. Place on an ungreased baking sheet and bake in a preheated 325°F. oven until just firm, about 10 minutes. Makes about 3 1/2 dozen.

MINTED MELONS

HONEYDEW	1/2 melon
CANTALOUPE	1/2 melon
WATERMELON	2 cups bite-size cubes
GRENADINE SYRUP	3/4 cup or 3/4 cup cranberry juice with honey or sugar to taste
SALT	1/8 teaspoon
MINT LEAVES	

Remove rind and seeds from the melons. Cut flesh into bite-size cubes and place in a bowl. Add GRENADINE SYRUP and SALT. Toss lightly; chill and garnish with MINT LEAVES. Serves 6.

ARARAT COMPOTE
Mixed Dried Cooked Fruit in Pomegranate Juice

DRIED APRICOTS	1/2 pound
DRIED FIGS	1/4 pound
DATES	1/4 pound
RAISINS	1/3 cup
PINE NUTS	1/4 cup
ALMONDS	3 tablespoons, slivered

PISTACHIO NUTS	2 tablespoons, chopped
HONEY	or sugar, 1/4 cup
POMEGRANATE JUICE	or cranberry
WATER	
POMEGRANATE SEEDS	optional

Combine the fruits, nuts and HONEY in a saucepan. Cover with a mixture of half POMEGRANATE JUICE and half WATER. Bring to a boil and simmer uncovered about 20 minutes or until fruit is soft; add more liquid if necessary. Cool and chill. When ready to serve, sprinkle with POME-GRANATE SEEDS. Any combination of dried fruit or liquid may be substituted. Serves 6.

MANNA PUDDING

BUTTER	3 tablespoons
DATE SUGAR	or brown, 1/2 cup
BAKING SODA	1/4 teaspoon
MILK	2 cups
EGGS	2, slightly beaten
SALT	1/4 teaspoon
ANISE	1/8 teaspoon
MACE	1/8 teaspoon
CINNAMON	1/4 teaspoon
GINGER	1/8 teaspoon
BREAD CRUMBS	stale, 2 cups
WALNUTS	1/4 cup, chopped, optional
RAISINS	golden, 1/4 cup, optional

Melt BUTTER in a saucepan; add DATE SUGAR and blend. Dissolve BAKING SODA in the MILK and add to SUGAR mixture; stir until blended. Add EGGS, SALT and SPICES. Fold in BREAD CRUMBS, WALNUTS and RAISINS. Pour into a greased 1 1/2 quart casserole. Bake in a preheated 350°F. oven for 30 minutes or until a knife inserted in the center comes out clean. Serves 6.

FROM THE GARDEN OF EDEN

LEAH'S PISTACHIO PUDDING

CORNSTARCH	1/4 cup
WATER	1/4 cup
MILK	2 3/4 cups, scalded
SUGAR	1/2 cup
ROSE WATER	2 tablespoons or 1/2 teaspoon almond extract
PISTACHIO NUTS	6 tablespoons, chopped

In a saucepan, mix CORNSTARCH and WATER together until smooth. Add hot scalded MILK and the SUGAR, stirring constantly. Cook over low heat, continuing to stir until thickened. It should resemble very heavy cream. Add flavoring and stir in 4 tablespoons PISTACHIO NUTS. Turn into a serving bowl; cover, cool and chill. When ready to serve, sprinkle with remaining PISTACHIO NUTS. Serves 4 to 6.

ANNA'S FAVORITE HONEY STRIPS

BUTTER	1/2 cup
HONEY	1/2 cup
EGGS	2, at room temperature, separated
CINNAMON	1/2 teaspoon
NUTMEG	1/2 teaspoon
MACE	1/2 teaspoon
DATES	1/3 cup, chopped
WALNUTS	1/4 cup, coarsely chopped
UNBLEACHED FLOUR	or all-purpose, 1 cup

Beat BUTTER and HONEY together until well blended and fluffy. Beat in EGG yolks, one at a time, until smooth and thick. Mix spices, DATES and WALNUTS with the FLOUR and add to the HONEY mixture. Whip EGG whites until stiff and fold into the batter. Grease an 8 × 8 × 2 inch square cake pan and turn in batter. Bake in a preheated 325°F. oven for 30 minutes or until a cake tester comes out clean. Let cool in pan for 10 minutes. Turn out and cut into 12 strips.

PISTACHIO NUT SOUFFLE

EGGS	5, separated, at room temperature
SUGAR	1/2 cup
FLOUR	3 tablespoons
SALT	1/8 teaspoon
MILK	1 cup, scalded
PISTACHIO NUTS	1/2 cup, coarsely chopped
BUTTER	2 tablespoons
ALMOND EXTRACT	1/2 teaspoon

Beat EGG YOLKS with SUGAR until light and lemon colored. Add FLOUR and SALT and blend. Beat in scalded MILK and cook over hot water, stirring constantly until it thickens and coats the spoon. Remove from heat and cool slightly. Lightly brown the PISTACHIO NUTS in the BUTTER and add to the eggs and milk mixture. Add the ALMOND EXTRACT. Beat egg whites until stiff and fold them into the mixture. Put the mixture into an ungreased, straight-sided baking dish and set it in a pan of hot water. Bake in a pre-heated 350° oven for 50 minutes until the soufflé is puffed and golden. Serve with whipped cream, if desired. Serves 6.

SARAH'S MELON JAM

MELON	cantaloupe, 2 pounds, peeled and seeded before weighing, cut into 1/2 inch cubes
WATER	1 cup
VINEGAR	white, 2 tablespoons
SUGAR	3 cups
SALT	1/2 teaspoon
GRENADINE SYRUP	or other fruit syrup, 1/4 cup

Put all the ingredients into a large kettle. Bring to a boil, turn heat down and simmer about 1 1/2 hours, until thick and transparent. Ladle into hot sterilized jars and seal with a 1/8 inch layer of melted paraffin. Makes about 4 half pint glasses.

NUT RAISIN PUDDING

BAKING SODA	1 teaspoon
SOUR MILK	1 cup
BREAD CRUMBS	soft, 2 cups, torn into very small pieces
BUTTER	1/2 cup
DATE SUGAR	or granulated, 1 cup
EGGS	2
ALMOND EXTRACT	3/4 teaspoon
UNBLEACHED FLOUR	or all-purpose, 1 cup
SALT	1/4 teaspoon
NUTMEG	1/4 teaspoon
RAISINS	1 cup, chopped
WALNUTS	1 cup, chopped
CREAM	heavy, optional

Add BAKING SODA to SOUR MILK; stir in BREAD CRUMBS and let stand 20 minutes. Cream BUTTER and SUGAR together until fluffy; add EGGS one at a time and stir in flavoring. Mix FLOUR, SALT and NUTMEG together and add to the BREAD CRUMB mixture. Stir in RAISINS and WALNUTS. Pour into a greased 1 1/2 quart baking dish; place in a pan of hot water, 1 inch deep. Bake in a pre-heated 350°F. oven about 40 minutes or until a knife inserted in the center comes out clean. Serve with whipped CREAM if desired. Serves 6.

FRESH FRUIT CAKE

FRUIT MIXTURE

SUGAR	2/3 cup
SALT	1/8 teaspoon
CINNAMON	1/4 teaspoon, ground
APRICOTS	or peaches, 1 pound, fresh, peeled, sliced
BUTTER	1/4 cup

Combine the first 3 ingredients and mix with the APRICOTS. Melt BUTTER in an 8 × 8 × 2 inch pan and add the APRICOT mixture; reserve.

CAKE

EGG	1 large, beaten
MILK	1/3 cup
BUTTER	2 tablespoons, melted
FLOUR	1 cup
BAKING POWDER	1 teaspoon
SALT	1/4 teaspoon
CREAM	heavy, whipped, optional

Combine EGG, MILK, and melted BUTTER; add to the sifted dry ingredients. Mix only until ingredients are blended; do not overbeat. Spread evenly over the APRICOTS. Bake in a preheated 375°F. oven until golden, about 30 minutes. Remove from oven and let stand 10 minutes before turning out onto a serving plate. Top with WHIPPED CREAM, if desired. Serves 6.

RAISIN NUT BARS

RAISINS	golden, 1 cup
WATER	1 cup
OIL	1/2 cup
SUGAR	1 cup
EGG	1
FLOUR	1 3/4 cups
BAKING SODA	1 teaspoon
SALT	1/4 teaspoon
CINNAMON	1 teaspoon
NUTMEG	1 teaspoon
ALLSPICE	1 teaspoon

CLOVES	ground, 1/2 teaspoon
WALNUTS	1/2 cup, chopped

Combine RAISINS and WATER and bring to a boil. Remove from heat and stir in OIL; cool and stir in SUGAR and EGG. Combine dry ingredients and beat into RAISIN mixture. Stir in WALNUTS. Pour into a greased 13 × 5 × 2 inch pan. Bake in a preheated 375°F. oven for 20 minutes or until cake tester comes out clean. Makes about 2 dozen bars.

ANGEL'S GRAPE SOUFFLE

GRAPE JELLY	3/4 cup
EGG WHITES	3, at room temperature
SALT	1/8 teaspoon
CREAM OF TARTAR	1/8 teaspoon
SUGAR	3 tablespoons

In a 1 quart saucepan heat the JELLY over low heat until melted; cool slightly. Beat the EGG WHITES until frothy. Add the SALT and CREAM OF TARTAR and add SUGAR gradually. Beat until meringue holds soft peaks. Fold about 2 cups of the meringue carefully into the JELLY; when well blended fold back into the remaining meringue. Spoon into an ungreased straight sided 1 1/2 quart baking dish. Bake in a preheated 350°F. oven for 20 to 25 minutes or until puffed and delicately golden. Serves 4.

GRAPE KETCHUP

GRAPES	Concord, 5 pounds
WATER	1/2 cup
SUGAR	5 cups
VINEGAR	2 cups
SALT	1 teaspoon
PICKLING SPICES	1/4 cup

Cover GRAPES with WATER; bring to a boil and cook about 3 minutes. Remove from kettle and spoon into a sieve. With a wooden spoon, press as much as possible through the sieve. Discard seeds and skins. Put pulp back into the kettle and stir in SUGAR, VINEGAR and SALT. Tie SPICES in a piece of cheesecloth and add to kettle. Cook slowly until thick, stirring often. Remove SPICES. Pour into hot sterilized bottles or jars; seal with lids at once. Serve with cold meats. Makes about 4 pints.

SPICED GRAPES

GRAPES	Concord, 4 cups, stems removed
WATER	1/2 cup
VINEGAR	1 1/2 tablespoons
SUGAR	2 1/4 cups
CINNAMON	ground, 1/2 teaspoon
CLOVES	ground, 1/2 teaspoon
NUTMEG	ground, 1/4 teaspoon
SALT	1/4 teaspoon

Wash GRAPES and drain. Slip the skins from the pulp; reserve the skins. Heat the pulp and boil 1 minute. Empty into a strainer and rub the pulp through. Combine the pulp, skins, WATER, VINEGAR, SUGAR, spices and SALT in a kettle and simmer 10 minutes. Remove, pour into hot sterilized jars and seal with a 1/8 inch layer of melted paraffin. Makes about 3 half pint glasses.

GOLDEN APPLE CONSERVE

APRICOTS	or peaches, 5 pounds, fresh
RAISINS	1/2 pound
DATES	1/2 pound, pitted, chopped
VINEGAR	2 cups
POMEGRANATE JUICE	or cranberry, 1/4 cup
SUGAR	3 cups
GINGER ROOT	fresh, chopped, 2 tablespoons or 3/4 teaspoon ground ginger

| WALNUTS | 1/2 cup, coarsely chopped |

Scald APRICOTS in hot water for 30 seconds; dip in cold water. Slip skins off and remove pits; dice. Put the APRICOTS and the next 4 ingredients in a large kettle. Cook over low heat until APRICOTS are tender. Stir in SUGAR, GINGER ROOT and WALNUTS and cook until thick. Stir often to prevent scorching. Pour into hot sterilized jars and seal with wax. Serve with curried dishes. Makes 10 half pint jelly glasses.

PICKLED SMYRNA FIGS

FIGS	fresh, 4 pounds
SALTED WATER	1/4 teaspoon salt to 1 cup of water
SUGAR	4 cups
VINEGAR	2 cups
CINNAMON STICKS	2, each 3 inches long
WHOLE CLOVES	1/2 teaspoon
GINGER ROOT	fresh, chopped, 1 tablespoon, optional

In a saucepan cover FIGS with SALTED WATER. Simmer 15 minutes and drain. Combine SUGAR, VINEGAR and spices in a kettle and bring to a boil. Add FIGS and simmer gently for 1 hour. Discard CINNAMON STICKS. Pack FIGS in hot sterilized jars covering them with the syrup to 1/2 inch of the top; seal with lids at once. Serve with cold meats. Makes about 3 to 4 pints.

CANTALOUPE CONSERVE

CANTALOUPE	1 1/2 pounds, peeled and seeded before weighing
WATER	1/2 cup
SUGAR	3 cups
SALT	1/8 teaspoon
GINGER	1 tablespoon chopped fresh or crystallized
RAISINS	golden, 1/4 cup
WALNUTS	chopped, 1/4 cup

Cut CANTALOUPE into 1/2 inch cubes and put into a

kettle. Add remaining ingredients and simmer until thick. Ladle conserve into hot sterilized jars and seal with a 1/8 inch layer of melted paraffin. Makes about 3 half pint glasses.

QUINCE PICKLE

QUINCE	7 pounds, unpeeled and cored
SUGAR	8 cups
VINEGAR	2 cups, white preferably
CLOVES	3 whole
CINNAMON STICK	1, three inches long
CORIANDER	1/4 teaspoon
ANISE SEED	1/4 teaspoon
BOILING WATER	2 cups

Cut QUINCE into 1/3 inch slices or in quarters. Simmer in a little water until tender. Drain and place slices in hot sterilized jars. Combine in a saucepan SUGAR and the remaining ingredients; boil over medium heat for 2 minutes. Pour over the fruit to within 1/4 inch of the top of the jar. Syrup should cover the fruit. Seal with lids immediately. Makes about 8 pints.

Note: Apple may be substituted for the quince.

WATERMELON JAM

WATERMELON RIND	3 pounds prepared rind
WATER	1 cup
SUGAR	6 cups
SALT	1/4 teaspoon
VINEGAR	2 tablespoons
GINGER ROOT	fresh, chopped, 2 teaspoons or 1/2 teaspoon ground ginger
CINNAMON STICK	1, 2 inches long
ANISE SEED	1 teaspoon

Remove red meat and use for melon balls. Peel off the green skin and discard. Finely chop white rind and drain; there should be 6 cups of pulp. Put pulp into a kettle with the WATER and remaining ingredients. Simmer over low heat until thick, stirring often to prevent sticking. Remove

CINNAMON STICK and ladle into hot sterilized jars. Seal with a 1/8 inch layer of melted paraffin. Makes about 5 half pint jelly glasses.

FORBIDDEN FRUIT JAM

APRICOTS   dried, 1 pound
WATER
SUGAR
VINEGAR   1 tablespoon

Soak APRICOTS overnight in WATER to cover. Empty APRICOTS and liquid into a saucepan and barely cover with WATER. Simmer uncovered until APRICOTS are very tender, about 20 minutes. Press liquid and pulp through a strainer. Measure equal amount of puree and SUGAR. Put puree, SUGAR and VINEGAR in a saucepan and cook over low heat, stirring constantly, until thick, about 6 minutes. Ladle into hot sterilized glasses; seal with 1/8 inch layer of melted paraffin. Makes about 4 half pint glasses.

GRAPE JELLY

GRAPES   Concord, slightly underripe, stems removed
WATER   1/4 cup for each quart grapes
VINEGAR   1/2 tablespoon for each quart grapes
SUGAR   1 cup for each cup dripped juice

Wash GRAPES and crush 2 cups in the bottom of a kettle. Add the WATER and boil gently for 12 to 15 minutes, until GRAPES are soft. Pour into a cloth lined strainer and allow to drip overnight. Pour the strained juice into a kettle and add the required amount of SUGAR. Cook until it reaches the jelly stage or 220°F. on the thermometer. Pour into hot sterilized jelly glasses and seal with melted paraffin.

GREENS OF THE EARTH

And God said, "Let the earth bring forth grass, the herb yielding seed."

GENESIS 1:11

As early as the third day of creation, God blessed man with abundant herbs and vegetables. This very passage has been used by famous Bible readers from St. Francis to George Bernard Shaw to argue that God intended man to be a vegetarian! The Old Testament is filled with stories of prophets and patriarchs who lived mainly on a diet of bread and a few vegetables. When Daniel was raised as a favored child in the King of Babylon's court, he "purposed in his heart" not to eat the King's meat, or drink his wine, but rather to dine on pulse (beans mixed with grain) and water. And even with that simple fare, Daniel and the other children's "countenances appeared fairer and fatter in flesh than all the children which did eat the portions of the King's meat"(Daniel 1:12–15).

Daniel's austere menu was adopted by most of the people since meat was a luxury eaten by the poor only on festive occasions. However, greens, lentils, cucumbers, onions and leeks were the staples that grew abundantly in the Holy Land. Whether mixed with herbs and seasonings, cooked into "pottage" or stew, baked with fish or eaten raw in leafy salads, vegetables more than any other food were the "meat" of our biblical ancestors. And although many other vege-

GREENS OF THE EARTH

tables which we savor today were unknown to them, the cooks of long ago made up in creativity for what they lacked in variety.

While we might think that this kind of diet was lacking in body-building healthful foods, the Bible proves that the multitudes thrived on their lean and leafy diet. Records of the ancient Pharoahs show that onions, garlic and radishes were fed to the Israelites while they toiled long days and nights to build the Great Pyramids. In all, the food bill for the vegetable-loving Hebrews came to over 4 million dollars in Egyptian silver!

Later, when the descendants of Jacob escaped from Egypt, they longed for the food they enjoyed in captivity which was as cool and refreshing as the desert was hot and barren: "We remember . . . the cucumbers, and the melons, and the leeks, and the onions, and the garlick" (Numbers 11:5).

The cool, moist, green cucumber must have been especially hard for the thirsty Hebrews to forget. Moses, walking along the banks of the Nile at Pharaoh's court, would have seen acres and acres of these green-vined and abundantly fruited vegetables growing in the rich mud of this river. The cucumber, which we enjoy today mainly as a side dish or in a salad, was one of the most favored of all foods, especially in the summer, when it was eaten raw. Often a meal of cucumber, melon and barley cakes was all that was available to the poor. So valuable was the cucumber, that small watchtowers were built in the vineyards and fields to protect the crops. It was to these frail lookouts that Isaiah refers when he warns the Israelites of the doom of the unfaithful: "And the daughter of Zion is left as a cottage in a vineyard, as a lodge in a garden of cucumbers, as a besieged city" (Isaiah 1:8).

The onions and garlic, so relished by the Israelites, were also widely grown in Egypt and Palestine, and were the main ingredients in many a folk tale and legend as well as many a cookpot. There is a tradition in the Orient that when Satan stepped out of the Garden of Eden after man's Fall, a field of onions sprang from the place where he put his right foot, and one of garlic from his left footprint.

Today we prize the onion for its flavorful pungency as a seasoning, but long before the laments of Moses' followers in the desert, it was a necessary nutriment. Sweet and soft, the onion was sliced into a tasty soup, or cut up and baked or eaten raw with fish and bread.

Some of the poor are said to have lived almost entirely on onions and bread. The wealthier folk enjoyed their pearly vegetables mixed with the meat of lamb, goat and sometimes chicken.

In Egypt the onion was thought of as sacred and as a symbol of the universe, since the spheres of the heaven, earth and beyond were said to be layered like an onion. According to old folk tales still alive, if a bunch of onions is hung in a crowded room, it will draw away the diseases of the people gathered there. It was also hung aloft much as we suspend mistletoe at Christmas time.

Garlic was popular in the time of Moses and there were many myths concerning it. It was reputed in ancient Greek legends to be good for the heart and for the making of love potions. These fragrant bulbs were considered a cure for a toothache, consumption, poisoned arrow wounds, dog bite and even recommended to reapers to strengthen their bodies against their strenuous work in the blistering rays of the sun. But the most important role of the sharp and spicy bulb was to mask foods on the verge of spoiling.

Hearty lentils and beans were vegetables most welcome in the daily diet. And so savory was the lentil soup which Jacob cooked for his older brother Esau, a meat eater and hunter, that Esau was willing to trade his birthright for a taste:

> And Esau said to Jacob, Feed me, I pray thee, with that same red pottage; for I am faint . . . And Jacob said, Swear to me this day; and he sware unto him: and he sold his birthright unto Jacob. Then Jacob gave Esau bread and pottage of lentiles; and he did eat and drink, rose up and went his way.
>
> Genesis 25:30–34.

The same kind of lentil which Jacob cooked in his "red pottage" abounds in Egypt and Palestine today. The lentil plants are grown in fields, then cut and threshed like wheat until the lentil "seed" falls away from its stalk. The seeds are then gathered, stewed, and eaten with bread.

Sometimes the poor made a kind of vegetable bread by mixing lentils, millet, barley and beans into "barley cakes." The beans referred to in all passages were fava beans, also called broad beans, and, because they were given to horses for fodder, horse beans. This was the homely fare that the fiery prophet Ezekiel prescribed for the Hebrews as penance during the fall of Jerusalem:

> *Take thou also unto thee wheat, and barley, and beans, and lentiles, and millet, and fitches [grasslike plants], and put them in one vessel, and make thee bread thereof, according to the number of days that thou shalt lie upon thy side, three hundred and ninety days shalt thou eat thereof.*
>
> *Ezekiel 4:9.*

Barley cakes every day for over a year—not exactly a gourmet's dream, but certainly nutritious! That is probably why David, the "sweet psalmist of Israel," also carried "wheat, and barley and flour, and parched corn, and beans and lentiles, and parched pulse" (II Samuel 17:28) when he led his army into the wilderness at God's command.

The "corn" described here and in many other Bible verses is not the Indian maize, the corn-on-the-cob we know today, but a vegetable mixture which included beans, lentils, barley and cumin. And the beans eaten by the followers of David were the same kind grown in ancient Egypt, where even today the bean fields waving by the shores of the Nile breathe the same sweet perfume which once inspired the poetry of Pharaohs.

Surely the leek, one of the vegetables the Hebrews missed in the desert with Moses, is treasured even more, for it has always been a food of the poor and a symbol of humility in the Orient. With a flavor sweeter and milder than the onion, the young leaves of this plant were eaten as a salad in old Egypt, where leeks are still grown in small backyard gardens and sold on the streets of Cairo. Our biblical ancestors might have diced the bulb into small pieces as a seasoning for meat, or eaten the leaves in a relish or soup as many Europeans do today.

Along with leeks, there were other salad foods often referred to as "bitter herbs." On their last night in Egypt, God ordered Moses to have the Hebrews slay young lambs and prepare a hasty meal with "your loins girded, your shoes on your feet, and your staff in your hand; and ye shall eat it in haste: it is the Lord's Passover" (Exodus 12:11).

"And they shall eat the [lambs'] flesh in that night, roast with fire, and unleavened bread; and with bitter herbs they shall eat it" (Exodus 12:8). The "bitter herbs" in the Lord's Passover that evening were undoubtedly the young leaves of chicory, sorrel, watercress, lettuce and dandelion—all weedy plants common in Egypt and still eaten by the Arabs as well as in the Hebrew Passover. The leaves were enjoyed raw in salads or cooked in soups or stews. The Egyptians blended these green potherbs with mustard and then dipped morsels of bread into the mixture.

Watercress and mint also were "bitter herbs." Watercress was a pungent plant related to the mustard family and eaten as a salad, boiled as a potherb or combined with raw or cooked vegetables. When mixed with vinegar, it was used as a remedy for madness by the Romans. This goes back to the Greek proverb, "Eat grass and learn more wit." So old is this herb's history that the name "watercress" dates back to the ancient Sanskrit verb meaning "to eat." Mint, in Greek writings, appeared when Pluto's wife changed the nymph Minthe into a mint plant. As a lowly mint plant she lost some of her beauty, but not her freshness or scent.

Some scholars doubt that the endive grew in Egypt and Palestine in the time of Moses. It was perishable and would not travel well so it could not have been imported. However, other interpreters believe it was native to Egypt, for it belongs to the chicory and escarole family which did grow abundantly there. One of the "bitter herbs" the Hebrews ate that first Passover evening was probably endive.

The gourd of the Bible has long been a source of mystery. When a water-weary Jonah sought shade in the desert after escaping the belly of the "great fish,"

> the Lord God prepared a gourd, and made it to come up over Jonah,
> that it might be a shadow over his head, to deliver him from his grief.
> Jonah 4:6

During one of the great famines, a follower of the prophet Elisha

> went out into the field to gather herbs, and found a wild vine, and
> gathered thereof wild gourds his lap full, and came and shred them
> into the pot of pottage: for they knew them not.
> II Kings 4:39

48

GREENS OF ThE EARTh

Was this wild gourd the pumpkin, the wintersquash, or the crook-neck? Although all are cultivated in Palestine today, the members of the squash family we know were native to the New World and not the Mid-East. The passage from II Kings 4:10 makes us realize that the gourd could not have been closely related to the squash family, because the pottage was so bitter and inedible that they cried out "there is death in the pot." Perhaps it was the colocynth gourd, also known as the bitter apple (it is reported that emperor Claudius was killed with its juice). In the Holy Land there is a legend that the prophet Elisha was so angry at the taste of the colocynth that he turned the gourds into stones which are still to be found on Mount Carmel where the round boulders resemble melons. Little wonder that the cooks of Bible times played it safe with leeks, garlic and onions.

A few wild ancestors of other vegetables are to be found in Bible verses. The thistle, when cultivated, became our artichoke. And the mallow, a rather salty green, was probably a forerunner of our own spinach.

But what of the many other vegetables we enjoy today—the egg-plant, carrot, potato, tomato, beet, and mushroom? None of these grew in the Holy Land during Bible times.

Carrots, along with many other root vegetables, were not referred to in the Bible or elsewhere until the third century BC. At that time only the feathery tops were considered fit to eat. Gavius Apicius, who lived at the time of Tiberius in the first century, gave directions for frying carrots and parsnips and serving them with a dressing.

Although the tomato was found wild by the Pre-Incas in Peru and Ecuador, nothing resembling the tomato was native to Asia, India, the Mediterranean area or Europe. This vegetable remained un-known to the Old World until Spanish explorers discovered it in South America and carried seeds across the sea in the sixteenth century. The size of the fruit then was probably no larger than the present day blueberry.

The children of Israel would never recognize many of the vegeta-bles that have been cultivated over the years from the first wild plants of the Holy Land.

CUCUMBERS AND RADISHES IN MINT DRESSING

SALT	1 1/4 teaspoons
CUCUMBERS	2, scored with a fork, cut in half lengthwise, seeds removed and thinly sliced crosswise
YOGURT	1 cup
HONEY	1 1/4 teaspoons
MINT	fresh, finely chopped, 2 tablespoons or 1 tablespoon dried and finely crushed
CHIVES	2 tablespoons, finely chopped
RADISHES	8, thinly sliced

Sprinkle SALT over CUCUMBERS; cover and chill for several hours. Mix YOGURT, HONEY, MINT and CHIVES together; refrigerate. When ready to serve, drain CUCUMBERS well and press out any liquid. Combine with the RADISHES. Strain the YOGURT mixture over the CUCUMBERS and RADISHES and toss well. Serve in a glass bowl. Serves 4 to 6.

SWEET AND SOUR PICKLED CUCUMBERS

CUCUMBERS	2 quarts or about 3 pounds, unpeeled and sliced 1/2 inch thick
ONION	1 medium, sliced
FENNEL BULB	1 medium, sliced, optional
GARLIC	5 medium cloves, cut in half
DILL	fresh, heads and stems, 5 each
VINEGAR	3 cups
SUGAR	3 cups
SALT	6 tablespoons
FENNEL SEED	1 teaspoon
MUSTARD SEED	1 teaspoon

Fill hot sterilized jars with CUCUMBER, ONION, FENNEL BULB and GARLIC. Place 1 DILL head and stem in each jar. Combine VINEGAR and the remaining ingredients in a saucepan and bring to a boil. Pour over the vegetables filling the jars to within 1/2 inch of the top; seal at once with lids. Makes about 4 half pint glasses.

GREENS OF The EARTh

PERGAMOS PICKLES
Spiced Sliced Cucumbers

CUCUMBERS	6 large, thinly sliced
ONIONS	6 large, sliced
SALT	1/2 cup
SUGAR	1 pound
VINEGAR	white, 1 quart
TUMERIC	powdered, 1/2 teaspoon
MUSTARD SEED	1/2 teaspoon
FENNEL SEED	1 1/2 teaspoons
GARLIC	5 medium cloves

Combine CUCUMBERS and ONIONS; sprinkle with SALT. Let stand overnight. Drain; rinse with cold water and drain again. Combine SUGAR, VINEGAR, spices and GARLIC in a kettle. Add the CUCUMBERS and ONIONS; cook, uncovered, over medium heat for 15 minutes. Ladle pickle slices into hot sterilized jars and fill to within 1/2 inch of the top with the hot liquid. Seal with lids at once. Makes about 5 pints.

KALE WITH HAM

KALE	or mustard greens, 2 pounds
HAM	1 pound, cooked, boneless, sliced 1/2 inch thick
MUSTARD SEED	1 teaspoon, ground
SAVORY	fresh, chopped, 2 teaspoons or 1 teaspoon dried
WATER	1 quart
BUTTER	2 tablespoons
SALT	
PEPPER	

Wash KALE, remove stems and tear in pieces. Cut HAM into 1/2 inch cubes leaving the fat on; if there is no fat, add enough butter or oil to fry the HAM cubes. Fry the HAM until golden and stir in the MUSTARD SEED and SAVORY. Add 1 quart WATER and the KALE; bring to a boil. Reduce heat, simmer covered, until tender; drain. Stir in BUTTER; SALT and PEPPER to taste. Serves 4.

CALAH CUCUMBERS
Cucumbers In Mint Dressing

SALT	1/2 teaspoon
PEPPER	freshly ground white, 1/4 teaspoon
OLIVE OIL	4 tablespoons
VINEGAR	2 tablespoons
MINT	1 tablespoon finely chopped fresh or 2 teaspoons dried
CUCUMBERS	2 large, scored, thinly sliced

Combine all ingredients, except CUCUMBERS, in a bottle and shake thoroughly. Pour over CUCUMBERS. Toss lightly and serve from bowl. Lettuce may be torn into bowl if desired, and tossed with CUCUMBERS. Serves 4 to 6.

BAKED FENNEL BULBS

FENNEL BULBS	3 large
BUTTER	1/4 cup
FLOUR	2 tablespoons
MILK	2 cups
SALT	
PEPPER	
ROMANO CHEESE	or Parmesan, 3 tablespoons, grated

Trim FENNEL tops and discard. Slice bulbs 1/4 inch thick and drop into boiling salted water; cook 5 minutes and drain. Melt BUTTER in a skillet and lightly brown the FENNEL slices. Remove to a shallow casserole. Add FLOUR to the remaining BUTTER and cook 1 minute. Stir in the MILK and cook until thickened. SALT and PEPPER to taste. Pour the sauce over the FENNEL and sprinkle with ROMANO CHEESE. Bake in a preheated 350°F. oven for 10 to 15 minutes or until golden and bubbly. Serves 6.

ENDIVE AND ROQUEFORT PLATTER

EGGS	2, hard-cooked, chopped
ARTICHOKE BOTTOMS	4, finely chopped
ONION JUICE	2 teaspoons

JAVAN DRESSING	p. 183, or mayonnaise
SALT	
PEPPER	
ROQUEFORT CHEESE	1 ounce
CREAM CHEESE	4 ounces
ENDIVES	6 leaves, separated and kept chilled until ready to serve.

Combine the first 3 ingredients and moisten with JAVAN DRESSING. SALT and PEPPER to taste; chill. Cream the ROQUEFORT and CREAM CHEESE together and chill. When ready to serve, form the CHEESE into a mound in the center of a serving dish. Place the ENDIVE leaves, which have been stuffed with the EGG mixture, radiating out from it. The ENDIVE leaves will lose their crispness if filled too long before serving. Serves 6 to 8 as an appetizer or 4 to 6 as a salad.

BETHANY BEANS
Baked Lentils

WATER	6 cups
LENTILS	2 cups
BACON	8 slices, coarsely chopped
ONION	1 large, chopped
SALT	1 teaspoon
PEPPER	freshly ground
SPICED DATE CHUTNEY	or any chopped chutney, 1/4 cup
MUSTARD	dry, 1 teaspoon
HONEY	1/2 cup

Put 5 cups WATER and LENTILS in a kettle and bring to a boil. Reduce heat and simmer, covered, for 1 hour. Drain off any excess liquid and reserve. Add to the LENTILS the remaining cup of WATER and the remaining ingredients except the HONEY. Turn into a 2 quart shallow baking dish and pour HONEY over the top. Bake in a preheated 350°F. oven, covered, for 45 minutes; remove cover; bake 30 minutes more. If LENTILS become dry, add some of the reserved liquid. Makes 4 servings.

ROMAN SPEARS
Artichokes With Curried Cheese Sauce

ARTICHOKES	4
VINEGAR	2 tablespoons
SALT	1 teaspoon
BUTTER	3 tablespoons
FLOUR	3 tablespoons
CURRY POWDER	1/2 teaspoon
MILK	1 cup
CHEVROTIN CHEESE	or Gruyere, 2 tablespoons, grated
CREAM	light, 2 tablespoons

Wash ARTICHOKES, trim stems, pull off tough outer leaves and snip off tips of remaining leaves. Place ARTICHOKES in 1 inch of boiling water to which 2 tablespoons of VINEGAR has been added. Sprinkle 1/4 teaspoon SALT over each ARTICHOKE. Cover tightly and cook 30 minutes or until stems can be easily pierced with a fork. Turn upside down to drain and keep warm. Melt BUTTER and blend in FLOUR and CURRY POWDER; cook 1 minute and gradually add MILK. Cook over low heat, stirring constantly; add CHEESE and cook until melted. Correct seasoning. Stir in CREAM. Serve the ARTICHOKES hot with the sauce. Serves 4.

CAPERNAUM THISTLES
Artichokes Stuffed With Chicken

ARTICHOKES	4
VINEGAR	2 tablespoons
SALT	1 1/2 teaspoons
CHICKEN	4 cups, cooked, chopped
CHIVES	2 tablespoons, chopped
TARRAGON	1/2 teaspoon chopped fresh or 1/4 teaspoon dried
MARJORAM	1/2 teaspoon chopped fresh or 1/4 teaspoon dried
PEPPER	freshly ground white
ROMANO CHEESE	or Parmesan, 1/4 cup grated

BREAD CRUMBS	dry, 1/4 cup
EGGS	2, beaten
MILK	1/4 cup

Wash ARTICHOKES, trim stems, remove outer leaves and snip off tips of remaining leaves. Spread and press leaves apart; remove center leaves and choke with a spoon. Place ARTICHOKES in 1 inch of boiling water, to which 2 tablespoons of VINEGAR have been added. Sprinkle 1/4 teaspoon SALT over each ARTICHOKE. Cover tightly and cook 30 minutes or until stems can be easily pierced with a fork. Remove and turn upside down to drain. Combine remaining SALT and remaining ingredients; mix well. Arrange ARTICHOKES in a deep 2 1/2 quart casserole. Fill with CHICKEN mixture. Bake covered in a preheated 350°F. oven for 20 minutes. Uncover and bake 5 to 10 minutes more. Serves 4.

LEEK SALAD

OLIVE OIL	1/2 cup
VINEGAR	tarragon, 1/4 cup
ONION	1 tablespoon, grated
CHIVES	1 tablespoon, chopped
SALT	1 teaspoon
PEPPER	white, 1/4 teaspoon
LEEKS	8 medium
PARSLEY	1 tablespoon, chopped
EGG	1, hard-cooked, chopped

Combine the first 6 ingredients in a bottle. Shake to blend well. Trim root ends of LEEKS; cut tops so they measure about 7 inches in length. Wash well and pat dry. Drop LEEKS into 1 1/2 quarts of boiling water to which 1 teaspoon SALT has been added. Simmer until fork tender; drain and cool. Place LEEKS in a dish in one layer and pour over the dressing. Refrigerate until well chilled. When ready to serve, remove LEEKS to a serving dish and sprinkle with PARSLEY and the chopped EGG. Serves 8.

GREEN ONIONS IN PARSLEY SAUCE

GREEN ONIONS	1 pound
STOCK	chicken, 1 cup
BUTTER	1/4 cup
ONIONS	yellow or white, 2 tablespoons, chopped
FLOUR	1 tablespoon
SALT	1/2 teaspoon
PARSLEY	2 tablespoons, finely chopped

Wash and trim GREEN ONIONS to about 6 inches. Place in a skillet, add STOCK and bring to a boil. Reduce heat and simmer, covered, for 6 to 8 minutes or until tender. Drain and reserve liquid which should measure about 3/4 cup. Arrange GREEN ONIONS on a serving platter and keep warm. Heat BUTTER in a small saucepan and cook chopped ONIONS until tender, about 5 minutes. Stir in FLOUR and SALT; add reserved liquid gradually and blend well. Cook 1 minute and add PARSLEY; pour over GREEN ONIONS. Makes 4 servings.

BAKED ONIONS

ONIONS	4 large, cut into 1/4 inch slices
BREAD	day old, 6 slices
ROQUEFORT CHEESE	1 cup, finely crumbled
CREAM	light, 1 cup
EGGS	3, beaten
DILL WEED	fresh, chopped, 1 teaspoon or 1/2 teaspoon dried
PEPPER	freshly ground, 1/8 teaspoon
BUTTER	

Boil ONIONS for 10 minutes. Remove crusts and cut BREAD into 1/4 inch cubes. Put drained ONIONS in a shallow 1 1/2 quart casserole and cover with BREAD cubes; sprinkle with ROQUEFORT CHEESE. Mix CREAM, EGGS, DILL and PEPPER together. Pour over ingredients in casserole; dot with BUTTER. Bake in a pre-heated 375°F. oven for about 40 minutes. Serves 6.

SPINACH IN CHEESE SAUCE

SPINACH	fresh, 1 pound
VINEGAR	1 tablespoon
EGGS	2, hard-cooked, sliced
BUTTER	3 tablespoons
FLOUR	3 tablespoons
MILK	1 cup
NUTMEG	1/8 teaspoon
CHEVRE CHEESE	or Swiss, 1/4 cup, grated
ROMANO CHEESE	or Parmesan, 1/2 cup, grated
SALT	
PEPPER	

In a large saucepan cook cleaned SPINACH, covered, over low heat for 5 minutes or until tender; stir occasionally. Do not add water; drain well. Turn into a greased 1 quart casserole; sprinkle with VINEGAR and arrange EGG slices on top. In a small saucepan melt BUTTER, stir in FLOUR and cook 1 minute. Gradually add the MILK and cook until smooth and thickened. Add NUTMEG and stir in the CHEVRE CHEESE and 1/4 cup of the ROMANO. Add SALT and PEPPER to taste. Pour sauce over the SPINACH and sprinkle with remaining 1/4 cup ROMANO. Bake uncovered in a pre-heated 375°F. oven until golden. Serves 4.

FENNEL SALAD

FENNEL BULBS	3 large
STOCK	chicken or water
ERECH DRESSING	p.182, or French dressing, 1 cup
EGGS	2 hard cooked, sliced
BLACK OLIVES	unpitted, 12, preferably Greek
WATERCRESS	

Remove coarse outside stalks and cut off tops. Split in half lengthwise and cook in STOCK to cover, until fork tender. Let cool in STOCK; drain. Marinate in ERECH DRESSING (p. 182). Serve on a bed of WATERCRESS. Garnish with EGGS and OLIVES. Serves 6.

SCALLOPED ONIONS

ONIONS	6 medium, thinly sliced
BUTTER	4 tablespoons
FLOUR	3 tablespoons
MILK	1 cup
SALT	1 teaspoon
PEPPER	white, 1/8 teaspoon, freshly ground
COTTAGE CHEESE	1 cup
GREEN ONION TOPS	2 tablespoons, finely chopped
DILL	fresh, chopped, 1/2 teaspoon, or 1/4 teaspoon dried
PARSLEY	2 tablespoons, chopped
BREAD CRUMBS	soft, 3/4 cup

Cook ONIONS in boiling salted water until tender, about 8 minutes. Melt 2 tablespoons BUTTER and stir in FLOUR. Gradually add MILK, stirring until thick; add SALT, PEPPER and COTTAGE CHEESE mixing well. Add GREEN ONION TOPS, DILL and PARSLEY; correct the seasoning. Arrange drained ONIONS in a shallow 4 cup buttered baking dish in alternate layers with the

CHEESE mixture; cover with BREAD CRUMBS. Dot with remaining BUTTER and bake in a preheated 350°F. oven for about 20 minutes or until bubbly and golden. Serves 4.

SALAD GILGAL
Radishes With Seed Dressing

VINEGAR	2 tablespoons, preferably tarragon
OLIVE OIL	3 tablespoons
SALT	1 1/2 teaspoons
PEPPER	1/4 teaspoon, freshly ground white
CARAWAY SEED	1/2 teaspoon
GARLIC	1 medium clove, finely chopped
RADISHES	1 1/2 pounds, thinly sliced
CORIANDER LEAVES	or parsley, 2 tablespoons, finely chopped

Combine the first 6 ingredients in a jar; let stand several hours. Toss with RADISHES 1/2 hour before serving. Sprinkle with CORIANDER LEAVES. Serves 6.

PICKLED ONIONS

WATER	1 quart
ONIONS	small, white, 2 pounds
SALT	1/2 cup
VINEGAR	white, 4 cups
SUGAR	1/2 cup
PICKLING SPICES	2 tablespoons
PEPPERCORNS	12

In a kettle bring WATER to a boil and drop in the ONIONS; return to a boil and cook 1 minute. Drain and pour cold WATER over onions. Peel off the skins and place ONIONS in a bowl; sprinkle with SALT. Cover and let stand 24 hours. Rinse in cold WATER to remove all SALT and pat dry with a paper towel. In a saucepan boil the VINEGAR and the remaining ingredients together for 5 minutes. Add ONIONS and cook about 10 minutes or until just tender. Remove ONIONS with a slotted spoon and put into hot sterilized jars. Pour the VINEGAR mixture over the ONIONS to within 1/2 inch of the top of the jars. Seal jars and let stand 2 weeks. Makes 2 one pint jars.

SQUASH FRITTERS

YELLOW SQUASH	4 to 5 inches long, 1 1/2 cups, unpeeled, finely chopped
EGGS	2, slightly beaten
FLOUR	1/2 cup
BAKING POWDER	1 teaspoon
SALT	1/2 teaspoon
DILL	fresh, 1 teaspoon, chopped or 1/2 teaspoon, dried
ONION	1 tablespoon, finely chopped
OIL	for frying

Drop SQUASH into boiling water and cook uncovered 2 to 3 minutes. Drain in a strainer and cool under running water. Drain again and pat dry on paper towel. Mix the EGG with combined remaining dry ingredients. Stir in SQUASH. Drop by tablespoonfuls into hot oil, 375°F., and cook until golden brown. Drain on paper towel. Serves 4.

VEGETABLES CARMEL
Spinach And Green Onions

SPINACH	3 pounds
GREEN ONIONS	3, finely chopped
PARSLEY	2 tablespoons, finely chopped
ROSEMARY LEAVES	fresh, chopped, 1 teaspoon or 1/2 teaspoon dried
BUTTER	1/4 cup
SALT	
PEPPER	

Wash SPINACH well and trim stems. In a large saucepan cook GREEN ONIONS, PARSLEY and ROSEMARY in BUTTER for 2 minutes. Add the SPINACH, toss with herb mixture and cook, covered, for 5 minutes or until limp. SALT and PEPPER to taste. Serves 6.

GREENS OF THE EARTH

CHALDEA CURRY
Vegetable Curry

DRIED LENTILS	1/2 cup
MILK	1 cup
ONIONS	1 cup, chopped
OIL	2 tablespoons
CORIANDER SEED	2 teaspoons, ground
CUMIN SEED	1/2 teaspoon, ground
FENNEL SEED	1/4 teaspoon, ground
MUSTARD SEED	1/8 teaspoon
ANISE SEED	1/8 teaspoon
CINNAMON	1/16 teaspoon
CLOVES	1/16 teaspoon, ground
GINGER	1/16 teaspoon
WATER	2 cups
SALT	1 teaspoon
PEPPER	1/8 teaspoon

Wash LENTILS, add to MILK and soak overnight in refrigerator. Cook ONIONS in OIL until lightly brown; add spices and cook 1 minute more. Stir in WATER, LENTILS and MILK. Bring to a boil; cover and simmer over low heat for 1 hour or until LENTILS are tender. Correct the seasoning. Serve over bulgur, millet or barley or as a side dish with chicken. Serves 4.

SPINACH BACON SALAD

SPINACH	fresh, 1/2 pound
WATERCRESS	1/2 pound
VINEGAR	3 tablespoons
SOUR CREAM	1/4 cup
OIL	1/3 cup
CHIVES	1 tablespoon, chopped
SALT	1/4 teaspoon
PEPPER	freshly ground, 1/8 teaspoon
BACON	8 slices, cooked crisp, chopped

Remove large coarse stems from SPINACH and WATERCRESS; wash and crisp. Beat the VINEGAR into the SOUR

CREAM very slowly; add the OIL a few drops at a time while continuing to beat until well blended. Add the CHIVES, SALT and PEPPER. Tear SPINACH and WATERCRESS into pieces; pour the dressing over and toss until all leaves are coated. Sprinkle with BACON. Serves 4.

HOT CUCUMBERS IN SOUR CREAM

CUCUMBERS	2, large, peeled, sliced 1/4 inch thick
SALT	
BUTTER	1/4 cup
ONIONS	2, medium, thinly sliced
CURRY POWDER	1 teaspoon
FLOUR	1 tablespoon
SOUR CREAM	3/4 cup, at room temperature

Sprinkle CUCUMBERS lightly with SALT and let stand 20 minutes. Heat BUTTER in a skillet and add CUCUMBERS and ONIONS; cook until both are tender. Stir in the CURRY POWDER and FLOUR and cook 1 minute more. Mix in the SOUR CREAM and heat but do not boil. Correct seasoning. Serves 4.

MARTHA'S MIXED SALAD

GARLIC	1 large clove, crushed
LETTUCE	1 head each, romaine and escarole, torn into pieces
CUCUMBERS	2 large, unpeeled, scored, thinly sliced
RADISHES	12, thinly sliced
GREEN ONIONS	6, cut into 1/2 inch pieces
OLIVES	12, black, pitted, slivered, preferably Greek
FETA CHEESE	or Roquefort, 4 ounces, crumbled
ANCHOVIES	4 to 6, flat, cut in half, optional
OIL	1/3 cup
VINEGAR	1/4 cup
OREGANO LEAVES	fresh, chopped, 1 1/2 teaspoons or 3/4 teaspoon dried
PEPPER	freshly ground

GReeNS OF The eARTh

Rub wooden salad bowl with GARLIC and add LETTUCE. Place CUCUMBERS around edge of bowl, RADISHES in the center and ONIONS on top. Ring the RADISHES with OLIVES. Sprinkle on the FETA CHEESE and cross the ANCHOVIES on top. Mix the remaining ingredients together in a bowl and pour over the salad just before serving. Toss well. Serves 8.

SQUASH PANCAKES

SQUASH	yellow, peeled, seeds removed, grated, 3 cups
SALT	2 teaspoons
EGGS	3
FETA CHEESE	1 cup, grated
MINT	fresh, chopped, 1 tablespoon, or 1 1/2 teaspoons dried
FLOUR	3 tablespoons
PEPPER	white, freshly ground

Mix SQUASH with SALT and let stand 1 hour. Squeeze out moisture. Beat EGGS; add SQUASH, CHEESE, MINT, FLOUR, and PEPPER to taste. Fry 1 tablespoon at a time over medium heat in a small skillet. Serve with butter or honey.

MIRIAM'S SPINACH SALAD

SOUR CREAM	1/2 cup
HONEY	2 tablespoons
RADISHES	2 tablespoons, grated
MUSTARD	dry, 1/2 teaspoon
SALT	1/4 teaspoon
VINEGAR	tarragon, 3 tablespoons
SPINACH	fresh, 1/2 pound, torn into pieces
COTTAGE CHEESE	1 1/2 cups
WALNUTS	1/2 cup, chopped

Stir the first 5 ingredients together and blend in the VINEGAR. Cover and chill. Arrange SPINACH in a salad bowl and top with COTTAGE CHEESE and WALNUTS. Pour on dressing; toss lightly to coat SPINACH leaves. Serves 6.

SQUASH AND ONIONS JONAH

YELLOW SQUASH	2 pounds, washed and diced
ONIONS	3 medium, thinly sliced
BUTTER	3 tablespoons
SALT	1/2 teaspoon
PEPPER	1/4 teaspoon
TARRAGON	fresh, chopped, 1 teaspoon, or 1/2 teaspoon dried

Combine all ingredients in a skillet. Cover and cook until tender, about 15 minutes. Serves 4.

ANTIOCH SALAD

Fava Beans In Oil Dressing

OLIVE OIL	1/2 cup
VINEGAR	tarragon, 1/4 cup
PARSLEY	1/2 cup, chopped
SALT	1 teaspoon
PEPPER	freshly ground white, 1/2 teaspoon
FAVA BEANS	or large lima beans, cooked, 2 cups
ROMAINE LETTUCE	
EGG	1, hard-cooked, chopped

Mix together in a bowl, OLIVE OIL, VINEGAR, 1/4 cup PARSLEY, SALT and PEPPER. Pour dressing over beans tossing lightly. Marinate at room temperature for 30 minutes, tossing several times. Serve in a bowl lined with ROMAINE leaves and topped with the chopped EGG and remaining PARSLEY. Serves 6.

STUFFED ENDIVES REUBEN

SMOKED BEEF TONGUE	or ham, 1/2 pound, cooked, finely chopped
EGGS	2, hard-cooked, chopped
SWEET PICKLE	1 tablespoon, chopped

PARSLEY	1 tablespoon, chopped
CHIVES	1 tablespoon, chopped
MUSTARD	dry, 1/2 teaspoon
JAVAN DRESSING	p. 183, or mayonnaise
SALT	
PEPPER	
ENDIVES	4 to 6

Mix TONGUE, EGGS and the next 4 ingredients together. Moisten with JAVAN DRESSING, SALT and PEPPER to taste. Separate leaves of ENDIVES and spread some of the mixture down the center of each leaf. Serve with dark bread and butter sandwiches.

LEEKS ROMANO

LEEKS	8, 1 to 1 1/2 inches in diameter, cut into 6 inch lengths, split in half lengthwise
WATER	2 cups
BUTTER	1/2 tablespoon
CREAM	heavy, 1/2 cup
SALT	
PEPPER	
ROMANO CHEESE	3 tablespoons, grated

Simmer LEEKS in WATER until crisp tender; drain. Butter a small casserole, add LEEKS and pour over CREAM; SALT and PEPPER lightly. Add ROMANO CHEESE and broil 5 minutes or until golden. Serves 4.

LENTILS AND OLIVE SALAD

LENTILS	1 cup
SALT	2 teaspoons
GINGER	1/2 teaspoon
MUSTARD	dry, 1/2 teaspoon
SHALLOTS	3 tablespoons, finely chopped
GARLIC	1 1/2 teaspoons, finely chopped
BLACK OLIVES	6 tablespoons, slivered, preferably Greek
VINEGAR	tarragon, 2 tablespoons

| OLIVE OIL | 5 tablespoons |
| PARSLEY | 2 tablespoons, finely chopped |

Rinse LENTILS; pour over boiling water to cover and boil 1 minute. Remove from heat and let soak 1 hour. Add SALT and boil over medium heat for 5 to 8 minutes; LENTILS should be crisp and firm. Drain, rinse under cold water and drain again. Spread on a paper towel and pat dry. Mix together GINGER, MUSTARD and the remaining ingredients. Pour over LENTILS and toss lightly; correct seasoning. Serve in a shallow bowl at room temperature, with goat cheese and crusty bread. Serves 4 to 6.

RED LENTILS

LENTILS	red, 1 cup
WATER	3 cups
TUMERIC	1 teaspoon
SALT	1 teaspoon
BUTTER	1/4 cup
ONION	1 large, thinly sliced
CUMIN SEED	1 teaspoon, ground
CORIANDER LEAVES	2 tablespoons, finely chopped

Wash LENTILS and add WATER and the next two ingredients. Bring to a boil, reduce heat, and cook until tender, about 20 minutes. Heat BUTTER, add the ONIONS and CUMIN SEED, and cook until tender. Drain LENTILS and combine with ONIONS. Correct the seasoning. Spoon into a heated bowl and sprinkle with CORIANDER LEAVES. Serves 4.

STUFFED THISTLE BOTTOMS

BUTTER	1 1/2 tablespoons
ONIONS	3/4 cup, chopped
SHALLOTS	or green onions, 3 tablespoons, chopped
BREAD CRUMBS	soft, fine, 1/4 cup
CHEESE	Chevre or Gruyere, grated, 1/4 cup

PISTACHIO NUTS   or pine nuts, .1/4 cup
SALT
PEPPER
WATER
ARTICHOKE BOTTOMS 12, about 1 3/4 inches in diameter

Cook ONIONS and SHALLOTS in BUTTER over medium heat until tender. Remove from heat. Add BREAD CRUMBS, CHEESE and NUTS; toss lightly with SALT and PEPPER to taste. Moisten with WATER and spoon onto the ARTICHOKE BOTTOMS mounding up in the center. Dot each one with BUTTER and place on a greased baking pan. Bake in a preheated 375°F. oven for about 10 minutes. Serves 6 to 8 as an appetizer.

BRAISED ROMAINE

LETTUCE romaine, including the white part, about 1 1/2
     pounds or any other type lettuce
STOCK beef, 3 cups
BUTTER 3 tablespoons
FLOUR 3 tablespoons
SALT
PEPPER

Separate leaves and wash ROMAINE thoroughly. Tear leaves into pieces and drop into a kettle of simmering STOCK. Cover and simmer 1 hour. Drain and reserve 1 cup of the liquid; save the remainder for a future soup. Melt the BUTTER in a saucepan and stir in the FLOUR. Cook 1 minute and gradually stir in reserved liquid; cook until thickened. Add cooked ROMAINE with SALT and PEPPER to taste. Place in a covered vegetable dish. Serves 4.

STUFFED SQUASH ELISHA

SQUASH yellow, 3 medium
ONION   1 large, finely chopped

BUTTER	1/4 cup
YOGURT	1/4 cup
CARDAMOM SEED	ground, 1/4 teaspoon
CREAM	heavy, 1 cup
ALMONDS	1/3 cup, blanched, ground
VINEGAR	2 teaspoons
SALT	1/2 teaspoon
CORIANDER SEED	ground, 1/2 teaspoon
PEPPER	freshly ground, white

Split SQUASH lengthwise and scoop out, leaving 1/2 inch thick shell. Chop SQUASH which has been scooped out, combine with ONION, and cook in 3 tablespoons of the BUTTER for 5 minutes. Add YOGURT and CARDAMOM. Cook 3 minutes. Add CREAM which has been mixed with the ALMONDS, VINEGAR and SALT. Cook 5 minutes more. Place the mixture in SQUASH shell; dot with remaining 1 tablespoon of BUTTER and sprinkle with CORIANDER SEED and PEPPER. Bake in a preheated 350° oven for 30 minutes or until shells are tender. Serves 6.

CURRIED ONIONS

ONIONS	4 large, sliced
OIL	1/4 cup
CURRY POWDER	1 teaspoon
SALT	1 teaspoon
PEPPER	freshly ground, 1/8 teaspoon

Cook ONIONS in hot OIL in a skillet until tender, stirring occasionally. During the last 3 minutes of cooking, stir in the remaining ingredients. Serves 4.

MANNA FROM HEAVEN

And there was no bread in all the land; for the famine was very sore, so that the land of Egypt and all the land of Canaan fainted by reason of the famine.

GENESIS 47:13

People of Israel were accustomed to hard times. Not always was the Holy Land the "land of milk and honey." In Egypt famine occured if there was any change in the rainfall and the proper overflow of the Nile. The most devastating famine recorded in the Bible was in the time of Joseph, who forecast the coming catastrophe by interpreting Pharaoh's dream of "seven empty ears blasted with the east wind" to mean there would be seven years of famine (Genesis 41:27). Other problems plagued the children of Israel in Egypt when the same "east wind brought the locust . . . they covered the face of the whole earth . . . and they did eat every herb of the land and all the fruit of the trees" (Exodus 10:13, 15).

Before they reached Canaan and were wandering in the desert, their hunger was severe. And God miraculously provided food: "And the children of Israel did eat manna for forty years, until they came to a land inhabited" (Exodus 16:35). Manna was probably an excretion from minute insects that ate the leaves of the tamarisk trees. It could be gathered each day after the dew had gone and before it was melted by the sun (Exodus 16:14, 15, 21). If it had not been for this

69

"bread of heaven," they indeed might have perished.

But there were good years when the fields brought forth abundant crops of grain. Wheat and barley were the most important grains grown throughout the Holy Land, and they have flourished in Egypt and Palestine ("a land of wheat and barley" Deuteronomy 8:8) since the dawn of time. In the Old Testament days, barley was more widespread than wheat, because it could grow in poorer soil and survive heat and drought better than any other grain. It was the universal food of the peasant and was considered a symbol of poverty and humility. King Solomon seems to have taken advantage of its rich abundance, since the laborers who built his lavish temple required a daily ration of more than twenty thousand measures of barley!

In Egypt and Palestine some wheat was trodden by oxen and pressed upon the ground by a cart wheel, just as described in Isaiah 28:28. Barley and other grains were threshed and winnowed by the farmer, and were usually ground into meal and flour by the women of the family, whose long day began before dawn when they heated the first fire for the daily work of continuous baking.

First, grain kernels from lentils, millet, barley or wheat had to be ground, usually with a kind of mortar and pestle approach, using a "rubbing stone" or a heavy handmill. The rubbing stone was really made of two slabs—one shaped almost like a saddle and often more than two and one-half feet long, and the second, a thinner, convex rock between which the grains were crushed. A handmill could also be employed in grinding. Here the upper stone had a wooden handle in the shape of a peg, which was worn smooth and had a hole in the center through which the grain was poured. This upper stone was rotated in a full circle by the handle, crushing the grain on a second stone beneath it. So important was the handmill to the survival of a family, that in the Book of Deuteronomy a creditor is forbidden from accepting a household's millstone as a pledge, because in doing so "he taketh a man's life in pledge" (Deuteronomy 24:6).

A fairly smooth-textured meal resulted from all this strenuous grinding. To produce "fine flour" favored by the palates of the rich or for sacred breads, this meal would be re-ground several times, or sifted through sieves until it resembled the packaged kind we buy today.

Sometimes the wheat was not baked into bread, but boiled without

MANNA FROM HEAVEN

being ground to make a thick kind of porridge, known as "burghul." Kernels of wheat and barley just harvested might be roasted on an iron plate or in a pan, thus becoming parched corn. These crisp kernels were carried in the pockets of the nomads on their long treks into the desert or eaten with bread as part of the everyday meal.

Abraham gives the first bread recipe in the Bible when he tells his wife Sarah to bake "a morsel of bread" (Genesis 18:5) for the three angels of the Lord who visit him: "And Abraham hastened into the tent unto Sarah, and said, 'Make ready quickly three measures of fine meal, knead it, and make cakes upon the hearth'" (Genesis 18:6).

In Old Testament times, breadmaking was well established as a profession, and the Hebrews probably learned the basics of this culinary art from the Egyptians. Found on the tomb of Rameses II (he was probably the pharaoh whose oppression led to the Exodus) is an interesting story in pictures of an Egyptian bakery and confectionary. On one side are two men leaning on staffs and kneading dough with their feet. In the center, a baker is stamping out animal and geometrically shaped dough for the fancy cakes. In another area, a pastry cook holds a spiral-shaped cake which he had just baked in an oven, much like our barbecue grill with a lid covering the wood fire.

For the simpler Hebrews, however, the ordinary loaf of bread was round with a diameter from five to sixteen inches. Some were "as thick as a finger;" others were thin as paper. For offerings, the bread was often cooked in pans.

Shewbreads were sacred and used only as an offering in the temple in the Old Testament. "Shewbread" or "showbread" or "the bread of the Presence" consisted of twelve loaves of unleavened bread which were always found on a long wooden table in the holy part of the temple open only to its priests. A symbol of God's abundance and grace, each week a fresh supply of this holy offering was baked and placed in the inner sanctum. It was this shewbread which the hungry David persuaded the keepers of the temple to feed him and his soldiers: "So the priest gave him hallowed bread, for there was no bread there but the shewbread, that was taken from before the Lord" (I Samuel 21:6). Later when the Pharisees accuse Christ and his disciples of eating food unlawfully and working on the Sabbath, Christ tells the story of David's taking of the holy offering: "Have ye not read, what David did, when he was an hungered . . . How he entered into the house of God, and did eat the shewbread" (Matthew 12:3, 4).

Unleavened bread was made by mixing flour, salt, and water in a wooden basin or "kneading trough." This dough was then molded by hand into flat discs and baked. These unleavened cakes were called "matstah" or "mazzah." It was just such bread which the Hebrews cooked in haste on the night of their escape with Moses:

And they baked unleavened cakes of the dough which they brought forth out of Egypt, for it was not leavened; because they were thrust out of Egypt, and could not tarry.

Exodus 12:39

Even today, during the eight days of Passover which commemorate the Hebrew's escape from bondage and the coming of the spring harvest, no bread or other leavened baked foods may be eaten in homes where this holiday is celebrated.

Usually, however, bread was allowed to rise, and a small lump of "starter dough" from the last day's baking was added to the new batch. The mixture was then set aside and allowed to ferment. Biblical cooks even had the equivalent of our commercial baking powder, which is made of soda, cream of tartar, flour and corn starch. Soda was obtained from the ashes of plants, and tartar from the crude substance found adhering to the sides of wine casks. The tartar was ground up, dissolved in boiling water and then filtered through charcoal. For a thickening agent which resembled our cornstarch, wheat starch was used. This was refined from three month wheat which was very light in weight.

As flavoring agents for their cakes and sweets, biblical people had a choice of ground almond, pungent grasses, seeds, herbs and fruit syrup flavored with spices. Sometimes the dough was mixed with olive oil and cumin seeds, with honey, cinnamon or saffron to add a little extra flavor and color.

Once the dough had risen, whatever its ingredients, there were three different ways to fire the bread. The "cake baked on the coals" for the prophet Elijah (I Kings 19:6) was prepared by the first and oldest method. First a few flat stones were gathered together and a fire was built upon them. After the stones were red-hot, the embers were raked off, the bread was laid on the stones and covered over with embers and ashes. After a while the ashes were removed and the cake was baked on the other side. When the demanding prophet Hosea rebuked the people of Israel for their wickedness, he used this baking style to describe the Israelite's leader: "Ephraim, he hath mixed himself among the people; Ephraim is a cake not turned" (Hosea: 7:8). And so, the next time someone comes up with a "half-baked" idea, you'll know the phrase comes piping hot from the pages of the Old Testament!

Bread was also prepared in another way, by placing a curved, bowl-like iron plate directly over a small fire built into the ground or in a small fireplace at the corner of a family tent. The uncooked bread was then placed on the metal and fired into steaming cakes. Even today the nomads of the Holy Land carry this portable "hot plate" or pan with them on their journeys through the desert.

Once the people of Bible times had settled down to become farmers and artisans, they used an oven called a "tannur" for their baking. In one type, heated stones were piled up and a large clay bowl oven was placed over them. Heat was applied from the outside and bread was baked on the stones within. A larger cone-shaped jar oven, and later a pit oven were also used for baking. Here the oven was heated by burning shrubs, twigs, dried roots, and animal dung, which were placed at the bottom of the oven. As the fuel burned, the cake dough was slapped onto the inside walls of the oven where it was quickly baked by the intense heat.

It was this last oven which was used by the professional bakers who flourished in those times. The services of these men were in such demand that there was a street in Jerusalem especially set off for their special trade. When the prophet Jeremiah was given royal protection, the king Zedekiah commanded that he should be given "daily a piece of bread from out of the bakers' street, until all the bread in the city were spent" (Jeremiah 37:21).

The bakers who once marketed their goods in old Jerusalem prepared a wide range of "bake meats" as described in the Old Testament—from the pancake loaf and flat barley cake to thin, waferlike disks of bread coated with honey or oil. For lighter confectionary treats, they whipped their dough and added eggs to their batter, often sweetening it with raisins and honey or flavoring it with pistachio and almond oils and nutmeats.

During the time when Christians began to worship openly in Rome, a dough was made consisting of flour, salt, and water. Bakers fashioned the dough into thin rolls, formed each into two arms crossed in prayer to remind them that Lent was a season of penance and prayer. They were called *bracalle,* the Latin word meaning "little arms." Many years later the Germans referred to them as *brezel.* They are known to us today as pretzels.

Bread was closely associated with Christ, not only because of his miracle of feeding the masses with five barley loaves (John 6:9), but from his birth. He was born in Bethlehem, which means "house of bread." Apparently, its name came from its location in the center of a productive grain area. Whether baked at home or brought fresh from the market place, bread was never cut, but always broken by hand. Christ often "breaks bread" with his disciples. Hot, savory bread rounds were served in light wicker baskets and morsels of the bread were given by the head of the household to the rest of the family and to guests. Bits of the broken bread were used almost like spoons to scoop out the hot food at mealtime. Most often this hot food was eaten from the communal bowl made of earthenware, wood, leather or copper. The Last Supper shared by Christ and his apostles began in just this way:

> *And as they did eat, Jesus took bread, and blessed, and brake it, and gave to them . . .*
>
> *Mark 14:22*

RUTH'S JOURNEY BREAD

JOURNEY STARTER DOUGH

YEAST	granular, 1 tablespoon
WATER	warm, 2 cups
UNBLEACHED FLOUR	or all-purpose, 2 cups

MANNA FROM HEAVEN

In a 1 1/2 quart glass or earthenware container, mix the YEAST, WATER and FLOUR together. Leave in a warm place for 48 hours; stir several times. It will ferment, bubble and smell slightly sour. To use, stir, then spoon out as much starter as recipe requires. Add equal parts FLOUR and WATER to remaining starter in container. Stir and let stand about 4 hours or until it bubbles again before covering and refrigerating. By replenishing the starter with flour and water it can be used indefinitely in the Journey Bread Recipe.

JOURNEY BREAD

STARTER DOUGH	1 cup
WATER	warm, 1 cup
UNBLEACHED FLOUR	or all-purpose, 4 cups
HONEY	or sugar, 2 tablespoons
SALT	2 teaspoons

Put STARTER DOUGH in a large bowl and mix in WATER and 2 cups of FLOUR. Cover and let stand 24 hours in a warm place. Work in HONEY, SALT and enough FLOUR to make a dough that will clean the sides of the bowl and can be gathered into a ball. Turn dough out onto a lightly floured board and knead 10 minutes. Cover and let rest 15 minutes. Divide in half and shape into 2 round or oval loaves and place on a greased baking sheet. Make diagonal slashes on tops of loaves, cover and let rise in a warm place for 30 minutes. Bake in a preheated 375°F. oven about 35 minutes or until crust is golden brown.

NAOMI'S LITTLE BREADS

Journey Biscuits

WHOLE WHEAT FLOUR	1 1/4 cups
UNBLEACHED WHITE FLOUR	or all-purpose, 1 1/4 cups
BAKING POWDER	2 teaspoons
SALT	1/2 teaspoon
BUTTER	1/2 cup
STARTER DOUGH	2 cups
HONEY	or sugar, 2 tablespoons

Combine the two FLOURS, BAKING POWDER and SALT in a bowl. Cut in the BUTTER until the mixture resembles coarse meal. Mix in STARTER from preceding recipe and HONEY; beat well. Turn dough onto a lightly floured board and knead for 10 minutes. Roll out to 1/2 inch thickness; cut with a 2 1/2 inch cookie cutter. Place on a greased baking sheet 2 inches apart. Cover and let rise 1/2 hour in a warm place. Bake in a preheated 400°F. oven about 20 minutes or until lightly browned. If all WHITE FLOUR is used, reduce STARTER to 1 2/3 cups. Makes about 32 "biscuits."

Note: Commercial whole wheat flour is so refined and tasteless that it is better to get the whole wheat and grind it to the desired coarseness. Put not more than 1/4 cup at a time into a blender. Start on low speed; after 30 seconds, move the switch to high. Stop the blender occasionally so it does not overheat.

DAYBREAK BREAD

BARLEY FLOUR	1 1/2 cups
UNBLEACHED FLOUR	or all-purpose, 1/4 cup
BAKING POWDER	1 1/2 teaspoons
SALT	3/4 teaspoon
MILK	1 1/2 cups
EGG	1, beaten
OIL	2 tablespoons

Mix the first 4 ingredients together in a bowl. Add MILK and EGG stirring in well. Add OIL and mix only until blended; batter will look lumpy. Preheat a greased 9 inch square pan in a 450°F. oven for 2 to 3 minutes before pouring in the batter. Bake 20 to 25 minutes. Cut into strips and serve hot. Makes 18 strips 4 1/2 × 1 inches.

SOUR MILK AND BARLEY BREAD

YEAST	granular, 1 tablespoon
WATER	warm, 1/4 cup
SOUR MILK	1 cup at room temperature
OIL	1/4 cup

HONEY	1/4 cup
SALT	1 teaspoon
BARLEY FLOUR	2 cups
UNBLEACHED FLOUR	about 2 cups

Dissolve YEAST in warm WATER in a large bowl. Stir in the SOUR MILK, OIL, HONEY and SALT; mix well. Beat in the BARLEY FLOUR. Add enough of the UN-BLEACHED FLOUR to make a dough that will clean the sides of the bowl and can be gathered into a ball. Turn out onto a lightly floured board and knead 10 minutes. Place in a greased bowl, turning to grease top. Cover with a cloth and let rise in a warm place until double in bulk, about 1 1/2 hours. Punch down and let rise 1 hour. Shape into 2 round loaves about 5 inches in diameter. Place on a greased baking sheet. Cover and let rise 1 hour. Bake in a pre-heated 350°F. oven for 30 minutes or until bread sounds hollow when tapped. Remove to a rack to cool.
Note: To make sour milk, put 1 tablespoon vinegar into a cup. Fill cup with sweet milk. Let stand a few minutes.

BREAD WITH WHEY

YEAST	granular, 1 tablespoon
WHEY	(liquid from curd of cottage cheese —see cottage cheese recipe) or water, warm, 1 1/4 cups
OIL	3 tablespoons
SALT	1 teaspoon
HONEY	or sugar, 1 tablespoon
UNBLEACHED FLOUR	or all-purpose, 3 1/4 cups

Dissolve YEAST in WHEY. Add the next 3 ingredients and half the FLOUR. Beat well; mix in the remaining FLOUR. Dough will be sticky. Cover with a cloth and let rise in a warm place until double in bulk, about 1 hour. Stir down and beat about 30 strokes. Put dough into a well greased 9 × 5 × 3 inch loaf pan. Cover and let rise until dough reaches 1/4 inch from top of pan, about 45 minutes. Bake in a preheated 375°F. oven about 30 minutes or until golden brown and bread sounds hollow when tapped. Remove to a rack to cool. If WHEY is used the bread has a flavor of sourdough. Makes 1 loaf.

UNKNEADED BREAD OF THRACE

YEAST	granular, 1 tablespoon
WATER	1 1/4 cups, warm
OIL	2 tablespoons
SALT	1 teaspoon
HONEY	or sugar, 1 tablespoon
UNBLEACHED FLOUR	or all-purpose, 3 1/4 cups

Dissolve YEAST in WATER; add OIL, SALT, HONEY and half the FLOUR. Beat well and mix in remaining FLOUR. Cover with a cloth and let rise in a warm place until double in bulk, about 1 hour. Stir down batter and beat a few strokes. Turn into a well greased 9 × 5 × 3 inch loaf pan; with floured fingers pat dough smoothly into the pan. Cover and let rise 1 hour. Bake in a preheated 375°F. oven for 40 to 50 minutes or until loaf sounds hollow when tapped. Remove to a rack to cool. Makes 1 loaf.

HONEYED GRIDDLE CAKES

STARTER DOUGH	1 cup
WATER	warm, 2 cups
UNBLEACHED FLOUR	or all-purpose, 2 1/4 cups
EGGS	2, at room temperature
HONEY	or sugar, 2 tablespoons
OIL	2 tablespoons
MILK	1/3 cup
BAKING SODA	1 teaspoon
SALT	1/2 teaspoon

In a large bowl mix together the STARTER, WARM WATER and UNBLEACHED FLOUR. Cover and let stand overnight in a warm place free from drafts. Next morning, beat in the EGGS and the remaining ingredients; let stand 10 minutes. Drop batter onto a hot greased griddle making pancakes 4 to 5 inches in diameter. Flip cakes when surface bubbles form. Makes 4 1/2 cups of batter or about 20 five-inch griddle cakes. Serve with HONEY SYRUP.

PALESTINE FOUR FLOUR BREAD

YEAST	granular, 1 tablespoon
WATER	warm, 1 cup
EGG	1, at room temperature, beaten
OIL	3 tablespoons
HONEY	1/3 cup
ANISE SEED	ground, 1 teaspoon
NUTMEG	ground, 1 teaspoon
SALT	1 1/2 teaspoons
MILLET FLOUR	1/2 cup
LENTIL FLOUR	1/2 cup
BARLEY FLOUR	1/2 cup
UNBLEACHED WHITE FLOUR	2 to 2 1/2 cups

Dissolve YEAST in warm WATER. Stir in EGG, OIL, HONEY, ANISE, NUTMEG and SALT. Mix in the MILLET, LENTIL and BARLEY FLOUR and beat well. Add 2 cups of the UNBLEACHED FLOUR. Mix well and add enough more to make a dough that will clean the sides of the bowl and can be gathered into a ball. Turn out onto a lightly floured board and knead 10 minutes. Place in a greased bowl turning over to grease top surface. Cover with a cloth and let rise in a warm place until double in bulk, about 1 1/2 hours. Punch down and let rise again for 1 hour. Shape into 2 round loaves, about 5 inches in diameter, and place on a greased baking sheet. Cover and let rise 1 hour. Bake in a preheated 350°F. oven about 30 minutes or until bread sounds hollow when tapped. Remove to a rack to cool. Makes 2 loaves.

Note: See instructions for grinding millet, lentil, and barley under Naomi's Little Breads.

REBEKAH'S GRIDDLE BREADS

YEAST	granular, 1 tablespoon
WATER	warm, 1/2 cup
HONEY	2 teaspoons
SALT	1/2 teaspoon
MILK	warm, 1/2 cup
UNBLEACHED FLOUR	or all-purpose, 2 1/2 cups
BARLEY FLOUR	or coarse meal

Dissolve YEAST in WATER. Measure HONEY and SALT into a large bowl and stir in the MILK and dissolved YEAST. Add the FLOUR and mix well. Turn dough out onto a lightly floured board and knead until dough is smooth, about 5 minutes, using more flour if necessary. Cover with a cloth and let rest for 10 minutes. Sprinkle board with a light layer of BARLEY FLOUR and roll out dough to 1/2 inch in thickness. Sprinkle more BARLEY FLOUR lightly over the dough. Cut with a 3 inch floured cookie cutter. Place each round on a piece of waxed paper. Cover with a cloth and let rise in a warm place, until double in bulk. Heat a heavy ungreased griddle or skillet over low heat. Place as many rounds as possible on the griddle, without crowding. Cook very slowly, about 10 to 12 minutes on each side, turning once, until browned. Remove to a rack to cool. To serve, split and toast. Makes 10 Griddle Breads. Note: Barley flour is the hardest grain to grind and takes a longer time in the blender. Grind not more than 1/4 cup at a time, starting on low speed and switching to high, stopping occasionally so motor will not overheat.

SEED BREAD

UNBLEACHED FLOUR	3 cups
BAKING POWDER	4 teaspoons
SALT	1/2 teaspoon
BUTTER	1/3 cup
SUGAR	1 1/4 cups
EGGS	2
MILK	1 1/4 cups
ANISE SEED	1 tablespoon

MANNA FROM HEAVEN

Combine FLOUR, BAKING POWDER and SALT. In a medium bowl cream BUTTER and SUGAR; beat in EGGS one at a time. Alternately beat in flour mixture and MILK, one third at a time, until well mixed. Add ANISE SEED. Pour batter into a greased 9 × 5 × 3 inch loaf pan and bake about 1 hour in a preheated 350°F. oven or until a cake tester inserted in the center comes out clean. Cool on a rack 10 minutes; remove from pan; finish cooling. Makes 1 loaf.

EZEKIEL'S MANY-FLOURED BREAD

YEAST	granular, 2 tablespoons
WATER	warm, 1 1/2 cups
EGG	1, at room temperature
OIL	5 tablespoons, reserve 1 tablespoon to brush top of breads
HONEY	1/3 cup
SALT	2 1/2 teaspoons
CUMIN SEED	ground, 1 tablespoon
CORIANDER SEED	ground, 1 tablespoon
LENTIL FLOUR	1/4 cup red or brown
BARLEY FLOUR	1/4 cup
FAVA or BROAD BEAN FLOUR	1/4 cup
MILLET FLOUR	1/4 cup
WHOLE WHEAT FLOUR	2 cups
UNBLEACHED WHITE FLOUR	1 to 2 1/2 cups

Dissolve YEAST in warm WATER. Mix in the next six ingredients. Stir in all the flours, with the exception of the UNBLEACHED WHITE FLOUR and beat well. Add enough of the UNBLEACHED FLOUR to make a dough that will clean the sides of the bowl and can be gathered into a ball. Turn out onto a lightly floured board and knead 10 minutes. Place in a greased bowl, turning over to grease top surface. Cover with a cloth and let rise in a warm place until double in bulk, about 1 1/2 hours. Punch down and let rise again about 1 hour. Shape into 2 round loaves and place on a greased baking sheet or in 2 greased 8 1/2 ×

4 1/2 × 2 5/8 inch loaf pans. Cover and let rise 1 hour. Bake in a preheated 350°F. oven for about 30 minutes or until bread sounds hollow when tapped. Remove to a rack to cool and brush with remaining tablespoon of OIL. Makes 2 loaves.

Note: See instructions for grinding lentils, barley, fava beans, millet and whole wheat under Naomi's Little Breads.

SINAI HERB BREAD

YEAST	granular, 2 tablespoons
WATER	warm, 1/4 cup
HONEY	1/4 cup
BUTTER	1/4 cup, melted
SALT	1 teaspoon
MILK	1 cup, warm
EGGS	2, at room temperature, slightly beaten
DILL WEED	2 teaspoons chopped fresh or 1 teaspoon dried
MARJORAM	2 teaspoons chopped fresh or 1 teaspoon dried
TARRAGON	2 teaspoons chopped fresh or 1 teaspoon dried
NUTMEG	ground, 1/4 teaspoon
UNBLEACHED FLOUR	4 1/2 to 5 cups

Dissolve YEAST in WATER. Mix in the remaining ingredients with the exception of the FLOUR. Add 3 cups FLOUR and beat well. Add enough of the remaining FLOUR to make a dough that will clean the sides of the bowl and can be gathered into a ball. Turn out onto a lightly floured board and knead 10 minutes. Place in a greased bowl, turning over to grease top surface. Cover with a cloth and let rise in a warm place until double in bulk, about 1 hour. Punch down, divide in half and shape into 2 round loaves or place into 2 greased 8 1/2 × 4 1/2 × 2 5/8 inch bread pans. Cover and let rise again until double in bulk, about 1 hour. Bake in a preheated 375°F. oven for 20 to 30 minutes or until loaves sound hollow when tapped. Remove to a rack to cool. Makes 2 loaves.

SPICED BREAD GALATIA

YEAST	granular, 1 tablespoon
WATER	warm, 1/4 cup
EGG	1 at room temperature, beaten
MILK	warm, 3/4 cup
OIL	1/4 cup
HONEY	3 tablespoons
CORIANDER SEED	ground, 1 tablespoon
CUMIN SEED	ground, 1/2 teaspoon
CINNAMON	ground, 1/4 teaspoon
SALT	1 teaspoon
WHOLE WHEAT FLOUR	2 cups
UNBLEACHED FLOUR	1 to 1 1/2 cups

Dissolve YEAST in warm WATER in a large bowl. Stir in EGG, MILK, OIL, HONEY, SPICES and SALT; stir in WHOLE WHEAT FLOUR and beat well. Add enough UN-BLEACHED FLOUR to make a dough that will clean the sides of the bowl and can be gathered into a ball. Turn out onto a lightly floured board and knead 10 minutes. Place in a greased bowl, turning to grease top. Cover with a cloth and let rise in a warm place until double in bulk, 1 1/2 hours. Punch down and shape into a round loaf about 7 inches in diameter. Place on a greased baking sheet; cover and let rise 1 hour. Bake in a preheated 350°F. oven for 30 minutes or until bread sounds hollow when tapped. Remove to a rack to cool. Makes 1 loaf.

THESSALONICA ONION BREAD

WATER	warm, 1 cup
YEAST	granular, 1 tablespoon
HONEY	or sugar, 2 teaspoons
SALT	1 1/2 teaspoons
OIL	1/4 cup
UNBLEACHED FLOUR	or all purpose, 2 1/2 to 3 cups
ONIONS	1 cup, chopped

Sprinkle YEAST over WATER, let stand 2 to 3 minutes and

stir to dissolve. Add HONEY, 1 teaspoon SALT, 2 table-spoons OIL and 2 cups FLOUR; beat until well blended. Add enough additional FLOUR to make a dough that will clean the sides of the bowl and can be gathered into a ball. Turn out onto a lightly floured board and knead 10 min-utes. Place in greased bowl, turning over once to grease top surface. Cover with a cloth and let rise in a warm place until double in bulk, about 1 hour. Punch down and divide in half. Put dough into 2 greased 8 inch round cake pans. Divide uncooked ONIONS and press lightly into dough covering entire top surface. Let rise in a warm place, uncov-ered, until double in bulk, about 1 hour. Brush with re-maining 2 tablespoons OIL and sprinkle with 1/2 teaspoon SALT. Bake in a preheated 375°F. oven about 25 minutes or until bread sounds hollow when tapped. Remove from pans and cool on a wire rack. Serve warm. Makes 2 loaves.

LEAVENED BREAD

YEAST	granular, 1 tablespoon
WATER	2 cups, lukewarm
SALT	2 teaspoons
OLIVE OIL	2 tablespoons
HONEY	1 tablespoon
UNBLEACHED FLOUR	or whole wheat, 5 to 6 cups

Sprinkle YEAST over lukewarm WATER; let stand 2 to 3 minutes and stir to dissolve. Stir in SALT, OLIVE OIL and HONEY. Beat in 3 1/2 cups of FLOUR and add enough remaining FLOUR to form a dough that can be gathered into a ball. Place on a lightly floured board and knead 10 minutes. Place in a greased bowl, turning over to grease the top surface. Cover with a cloth and let rise in a warm place until dough is double in bulk, about 1 hour. Punch down, form into a ball and cut into 8 equal pieces. Roll out each one to 1/4 inch thickness, about 6 inches in diameter. Place on a baking sheet, cover and let rise 45 minutes. Bake in a preheated 500°F. oven for 10 to 12 minutes or until golden. If oven has cooled due to opening door, return to 500°F.

before putting in the next batch. Remove from oven and wrap in a towel until ready to serve. The loaves will be puffed and have a pocket of air in the center. Makes 8 loaves.

DAVID'S RESCUE
Leavened Shewbread

YEAST	granular, 2 tablespoons
WATER	1/2 cup, warm
BUTTER	3 tablespoons, soft
HONEY	3 tablespoons, or sugar
SALT	2 teaspoons
MILK	1 1/4 cups, warm
BUCKWHEAT GROATS	or cracked wheat, 1/2 cup
UNBLEACHED FLOUR	or all-purpose, 4 to 5 cups
OIL	

Dissolve YEAST in warm WATER; mix in the next 4 ingredients. Stir in the BUCKWHEAT GROATS and 2 cups of the UNBLEACHED FLOUR and beat well. Add enough of the remaining FLOUR to make a dough that will clean the sides of the bowl and can be gathered into a ball. Place in a greased bowl, turning over to grease the top. Cover with a cloth and let rise in a warm place until double in bulk, about 1 hour. Punch down and turn out onto a lightly floured board. Cover with a cloth and let rise on the board for 15 minutes. Form into a ball and divide in half. Divide each half into 6 wedges and form each into a ball. Place on 2 greased baking sheets. Press flat to make a loaf about 3 1/2 inches in diameter; space 3 inches apart. Brush tops with OIL. Cover and let rise 1 hour. Bake in a preheated 375°F. oven about 20 minutes or until golden. Remove from oven and brush tops again with OIL; place on wire racks. Serve warm with butter. Makes 12 shewbreads.

GOLAN DISCS
Unleavened Bread

UNBLEACHED FLOUR	4 cups
SALT	1 teaspoon
WATER	1 1/2 cups, at room temperature

Combine the FLOUR and SALT. Add enough WATER to make a dough that will clean the sides of the bowl and can be gathered into a ball. Turn out onto a lightly floured board and knead 10 minutes. Shape into a ball and cut in half. Cut each half into 8 pieces and form into 16 balls. Roll out each ball to form about a 7 inch circle. Place on an ungreased baking sheet and bake in a preheated 500°F. oven for 5 minutes or until discs are lightly colored, blistered and crisp. Serve with cheese, dips, and soups. Makes 16 discs.

CAESAREA THINS
Unleavened Shewbread

WATER	warm, 1 1/2 cups
OIL	3 tablespoons
HONEY	3 tablespoons
SALT	1 tablespoon
BUCKWHEAT GROATS	1/4 cup
UNBLEACHED FLOUR	or all-purpose, 3 3/4 to 4 cups

In a bowl mix the first 5 ingredients together. Add half of the UNBLEACHED FLOUR and beat well. Mix in enough of the remaining FLOUR to make a dough that will clean the sides of the bowl and can be gathered into a ball. Turn out onto a lightly floured board and knead 10 minutes. Shape into a ball and cut in half; cut each half into 6 equal pieces. Form the 12 pieces into balls and roll each out to 1/16 inch thickness. Cut with a 1 3/4 inch cookie cutter. Roll each circle again to measure about 3 inches in diameter; they must be very thin. Place on an ungreased baking sheet in a preheated 375°F. oven for 3 to 5 minutes or until

sheep and goat cheeses   assorted breads   walnuts   David's Rescue Shewbread   olives

he fields brought forth abundant grains

Duck Phenicia

delicacy for peasants and kings

Stuffed Grape Leaves   Salad Gilgal   Cucumbers with Walnut Dressing   Tender Thistles   Pistachio Nu

days of feasting and song

*to delight the most
distinguished palates*

Chicken in Sour Cream

with the sweetness of man

Sweetmeats

d the flavor of chocolate

Lamb Casserole

eating was always
accompanied by thanksgiving

the edges are brown. Serve with cheese, dips and soup. Makes about 12 dozen.

HERDSMAN'S CAKE

UNBLEACHED FLOUR	2 1/3 cups
BAKING POWDER	1 1/2 teaspoons
NUTMEG	1/4 teaspoon
CARAWAY SEEDS	2 teaspoons
BUTTER	2/3 cup
DATE SUGAR	or brown, 2/3 cup
EGGS	2
MILK	2/3 cup

Combine the first 4 ingredients in a bowl and cut in BUTTER until mixture resembles coarse meal; mix in DATE SUGAR. Beat EGGS and MILK together in a small bowl; stir into flour mixture; do not beat. Pour into a greased 8 1/2 × 4 1/2 × 2 5/8 inch pan. Bake in a preheated 350°F. oven about 50 minutes or until cake tester comes out clean. Remove to a cake rack and serve slightly warm, cut into thin slices. Serve with a soft cheese.

APRICOT NUT BREAD

APRICOTS	dried, 1/2 cup
SUGAR	3/4 cup
BAKING POWDER	5 teaspoons
BAKING SODA	1/2 teaspoon
SALT	1/2 teaspoon
UNBLEACHED FLOUR	2 1/4 cups
EGG	1, well beaten
BUTTERMILK	1 cup
OIL	1 tablespoon
PISTACHIO NUTS	or walnuts, 1 cup, chopped

Cut APRICOTS into thin slivers. Combine the next 5 ingredients reserving 2 tablespoons of FLOUR to dredge APRICOTS and NUTS. Mix the EGG with BUTTERMILK and OIL and add to dry ingredients, stirring only until mixed. Fold in the dredged APRICOTS and NUTS. Spoon into a greased 9 × 5 × 3 inch loaf pan. Bake in a preheated 350°F. oven for about an hour or until a cake tester inserted in the center comes out clean. Turn out onto a rack to cool. Makes 1 loaf.

Note: This bread slices better the second day.

"LITTLE ARMS" PRETZELS

WATER	1 1/2 cups, warm
YEAST	1 tablespoon
SUGAR	1/4 cup
UNBLEACHED FLOUR	4 1/2 cups
EGG	1, beaten with 2 teaspoons water
SALT	coarse

Stir together WATER, YEAST and SUGAR in a large bowl. Let stand 1 hour. Mix in FLOUR thoroughly. Turn dough out on lightly floured surface and knead 10 minutes. Grease bowl, return dough to bowl, turning to grease the top. Cover and set in a warm place to rise until double in size, about 1 1/2 hours. Punch down, then pinch off a piece of dough about the size of a golf ball. Roll dough with hands to 15 inches long or pull into a smooth rope. Make a loop by picking up and crossing the ends of the rolled strips. Bring the left end of the strip over to the right and then the right end over to the left. This forms a twist in the center. Bring the ends up and over and press them against the sides of the loop, making the traditional pretzel shape. Place the pretzels on greased cookie sheets two inches apart. In a small bowl, beat EGG with water and brush on each one. Sprinkle with coarse SALT. Let dough rise again, 1/2 to 3/4 hour. Bake in a preheated 475°F. oven 10 to 12 minutes until golden. Cool on rack. Makes about 2 dozen.

Note: These pretzels can also be made in stick form.

MANNA FROM hEAVEN

TEA BREAD PHENICE

UNBLEACHED FLOUR	or all-purpose, 1 cup
WHOLE WHEAT FLOUR	1 cup
BAKING POWDER	1 teaspoon
BAKING SODA	1 teaspoon
SALT	1/8 teaspoon
EGG	1
BUTTERMILK	3/4 cup
SOUR CREAM	1/4 cup
GRENADINE SYRUP	or maple, 3/4 cup

Combine the first 5 ingredients. Mix the EGG and the remaining ingredients together. Stir the liquid ingredients slowly into the dry and mix well. Pour into a greased 8 1/2 × 4 1/2 × 2 5/8 inch cake pan and bake in a preheated 325°F. oven for about 1 hour or until cake tester comes out clean. Let cool in pan 10 minutes before removing to a rack.

DATE NUT BREAD

WATER	warm, 1/4 cup
YEAST	granular, 1 tablespoon
MILK	warm, 1 cup
HONEY	or sugar, 1 tablespoon
SALT	1 teaspoon
CINNAMON	1 teaspoon, ground
OIL	2 tablespoons
WHOLE WHEAT FLOUR	1/2 cup
UNBLEACHED FLOUR	2 to 2 1/2 cups
DATES	or raisins, 1/2 cup, chopped
PINE NUTS	or walnuts, 1/2 cup, coarsely chopped

Sprinkle YEAST over WATER; let stand 2 to 3 minutes and stir until dissolved. Add MILK, HONEY, SALT, CINNAMON and 1 1/2 tablespoons OIL. Stir in WHOLE WHEAT FLOUR and 1 cup of the UNBLEACHED FLOUR and beat well. Add DATES and NUTS and enough additional UNBLEACHED FLOUR to make a dough that will clean the sides of the bowl and can be gathered into a ball. Turn out onto a lightly floured board and knead 10 minutes. Cover dough on board with a cloth and let rest 20 minutes; punch dough down and divide in half. Form into 2 loaves and place in 2 greased 7 3/8 × 3 5/8 × 2 1/4 inch loaf pans. Cover with a cloth and let rise in a warm place until double in bulk or until dough reaches the top of the pan. Bake in a preheated 375°F. oven for about 25 to 30 minutes or until bread sounds hollow when tapped. Brush with remaining OIL and remove to a rack to cool. Makes 2 loaves.

BUTTERMILK PANCAKES

WHOLE WHEAT FLOUR	1 cup
BAKING POWDER	1 teaspoon
BAKING SODA	1/2 teaspoon
SALT	1 teaspoon
SUGAR	1 teaspoon
EGGS	2, separated
OIL	2 tablespoons
BUTTERMILK	2 cups

Combine the first 5 ingredients in a bowl. Beat the EGG yolks, add the OIL and BUTTERMILK; combine with the dry ingredients. Beat the EGG whites until stiff and fold in. Drop the batter by tablespoonfuls onto a hot greased griddle; when they are golden on one side, turn. Serve with honey. Makes about 30 pancakes.

SOUR CREAM PANCAKES

UNBLEACHED FLOUR	or all-purpose, 1/2 cup
BAKING POWDER	1/2 teaspoon
SUGAR	1 teaspoon
ANISE SEED	1 teaspoon
SALT	1/2 teaspoon
EGGS	2, beaten
SOUR CREAM	1/2 cup
CREAMED COTTAGE CHEESE	1/2 cup

Mix the dry ingredients together; add the beaten EGGS

and stir in the SOUR CREAM and COTTAGE CHEESE.
Cook on a hot greased griddle or skillet, turning once after
bubbles form. Serve with HONEY SYRUP (p. 91). Makes
about 16 three inch pancakes.

HONEY SYRUP

WATER 1 cup
SUGAR 1 cup
HONEY 1/4 cup

Bring WATER, SUGAR and HONEY to a boil and simmer
over low heat 30 minutes. Cool. Makes 1 1/4 cups.

BETHLEHEM BARLEY AND ONIONS

BARLEY 1 cup
BUTTER 3 tablespoons
ONIONS 1 cup, finely chopped
STOCK beef, 3 cups
SALT
PEPPER

Heat BARLEY in a dry skillet until it becomes lightly colored and has a nutty fragrance. Add the next 3 ingredients.
Cover tightly and simmer 50 to 60 minutes or until liquid
is absorbed and BARLEY is tender. SALT and PEPPER to
taste. Serve with lamb or fowl. Serves 6 to 8

FIRMITY

Joseph's Gift To Benjamin

BUCKWHEAT GROATS or kasha, 1 cup
MILK 2 cups
SALT 1 teaspoon
GREEN ONIONS 1/2 cup, chopped
HONEY 1/4 cup
BUTTER 3 tablespoons

Combine BUCKWHEAT GROATS and MILK in a saucepan; add the next 3 ingredients. Cover tightly and cook 20

minutes over low heat. Stir several times during the cooking to keep from sticking. Remove the cover and cook 5 minutes more. Stir in BUTTER; correct the seasoning. Serve with meat. Serves 4 to 6.

Note: Firmity was a dish of hulled wheat boiled in milk and reputed to have been sent by Joseph to Benjamin.

TARSUS PIE
Millet With Cheese Sauce

WATER	4 1/2 cups
SALT	1 1/2 teaspoons
NUTMEG	freshly grated, 1/8 teaspoon
MILLET	1 1/2 cups, ground
SAUCE FOR SAUL	

Bring WATER to a boil and stir in SALT, NUTMEG and the MILLET gradually so the WATER does not stop boiling. Reduce heat and continue cooking, uncovered, stirring occasionally until the MILLET is very thick, about 1 hour. Pour into a well greased 9 inch pie plate; cool and refrigerate until firm. Prepare sauce.

SAUCE FOR SAUL

BUTTER	3 tablespoons
FLOUR	3 1/2 tablespoons
MILK	1 1/2 cups
SALT	1/4 teaspoon
ROMANO CHEESE	grated, 1/2 cup

Melt BUTTER in saucepan. Stir in FLOUR and cook for 1 minute. Add MILK slowly and stir until smooth and thickened. Add SALT; reserve. Turn the MILLET out onto a flat surface and split in half horizontally. Return bottom half to pie plate and spread over one half the SAUCE FOR SAUL. Replace top half and pour over the remaining sauce. Sprinkle with grated ROMANO CHEESE and bake for 20 minutes in a 400°F. oven. Put under the broiler a few seconds until golden. Serves 4 to 6.

MILLET JUDEA
Millet With Nuts And Raisins

MILLET	1 cup
CHICKEN STOCK	3 cups
ONION	1 cup, chopped
BUTTER	1/4 cup
SALT	1 teaspoon
GOLDEN RAISINS	1/4 cup
PISTACHIO NUTS	or almonds, toasted and slivered, 1/4 cup

Toast MILLET in an ungreased skillet over medium heat, stirring constantly, for 3 or 4 minutes or until golden. Add remaining ingredients except the nuts. Tightly cover and simmer over low heat for 15 minutes or until MILLET is tender and STOCK is absorbed. Stir in NUTS and toss lightly. Correct seasoning. Serve with game or poultry. Serves 6.

"CORN"

ONIONS	1 cup, chopped
BUTTER	6 tablespoons
LENTILS	1/4 cup
BARLEY	1/4 cup
MILLET	1/4 cup
CRACKED WHEAT	1/4 cup
CUMIN SEED	1/4 teaspoon, ground
SALT	3/4 teaspoon
WATER	2 cups

In a medium-sized saucepan, cook the ONIONS in BUTTER until golden; add the remaining ingredients. Cover with a tight fitting lid and cook over low heat for 20 minutes; remove the cover and cook 5 minutes more. Stir several times during the cooking to prevent sticking. The WATER should be absorbed and the grain tender. Serve with meat or fowl with or without gravy. Serves 4 to 6.
Note: "Corn" in biblical times meant a mixture of lentils, barley, millet, wheat and cumin.

ABRAM'S SUPPER
Cracked Wheat And Bacon

CRACKED WHEAT	1 cup
BACON	8 slices, cut into 1/2 inch pieces
ONION	1 1/2 cups, chopped
WATER	2 cups
SALT	1/2 teaspoon
BUTTER	2 tablespoons
EGGS	2, hard-cooked, chopped
PARSLEY	2 tablespoons, chopped

Toast CRACKED WHEAT in a dry saucepan over low heat, shaking pan and stirring to prevent burning, for 5 to 8 minutes. In a skillet cook BACON pieces until crisp; remove and drain on a paper towel. Cook ONIONS until golden in the BACON fat. Add the ONIONS and fat to the toasted CRACKED WHEAT; stir in WATER and SALT. Cover tightly and cook 20 minutes. Stir several times during the cooking to keep from sticking. Remove cover and cook 5 minutes more. Stir in BUTTER and chopped EGGS; toss well and correct seasoning. Sprinkle with PARSLEY and BACON. Serve with cold meats and a salad. Serves 4 to 6.

the LANO
OF MiLk ANO hONEy

. . . the hills shall flow with milk.
JOEL 3:18

. . . for we have treasures in the field . . . of honey.
JEREMIAH 41:8

So common is the Old Testament expression "flowing with milk and honey," that scholars believe it was an early Palestinian phrase, rather than a description of any land. These two ingredients meant riches no matter where they were found.

Milk was usually stored in goat skins. When fresh milk was added to the leftover milk, it became slightly sour and sometimes fermented into "leben." By rocking the filled goat skin back and forth until butter appeared at the opening, women accomplished the "churning of milk [which] bringeth forth butter" (Proverbs 30:33). The newly made butter soon became rancid because of the hot climate; in order to be kept for any length of time it had to be boiled. The end result was called "samn," which is known to us as clarified butter. Salt was not used as a keeping agent for butter, although it was used as a seasoning.

Honey, just as much as milk, was a treasure when it was found: "all they of the land came to a wood; and there was honey upon the ground . . . and dipped it in an honeycomb" (I Samuel 14:25–27). Wild honey was first found in rocks and trees and in the carcases of animals (Judges 14:8); later beekeeping became popular. The honey and the comb were widely sought; both were eaten not only alone, but also added to drinks, used in cooking, and valued for medicinal properties. Honey was a welcome gift: "take of the best fruits in the land in your vessel and carry down the man a little honey" (Genesis 43:11). Other varieties besides bee honey were savored, those made from grapes, dates, figs and raisins. Sugar was unknown at that time, although it was later imported for the tables of kings. Fresh fruits and nuts were the sweets of the average person, but the cooks of the wealthy made sweetmeats with imported sugar and flavored them with essences from ginger and other herbs.

CHEESE SOUFFLE

BUTTER	2 tablespoons
FLOUR	3 tablespoons
MUSTARD	dry, 1/4 teaspoon
MILK	1 cup
CHEESE	Bryndza, 3/4 cup, crumbled or Roquefort cheese
ONION	grated, 2 teaspoons, optional
EGGS	3, separated, at room temperature

Melt BUTTER in a saucepan over low heat; stir in FLOUR and MUSTARD. Add the MILK and cook, stirring constantly, until thickened. Mix in CHEESE and grated ONION and stir until CHEESE is melted. Remove from heat and add the EGG yolks one at a time, stirring well after each addition. Fold in the stiffly beaten EGG whites. Pour into an ungreased 1 quart souffle dish or a casserole with straight sides. Bake in a preheated 350°F. oven about 30 minutes or until puffed and golden. Serves 4.

HOME MADE COTTAGE CHEESE

Pour 2 quarts of cow or goat MILK into a porcelain or stainless steel saucepan and heat to 110°F. on a thermometer or quite warm to the touch. Pour into a bowl; wrap the bottom and outside with a dish cloth and cover the top; place in the oven. If there is a pilot light it will keep the milk at the correct temperature; if not, place a 4 quart covered kettle of boiling water in the oven and reheat when necessary. Depending on the warmth of the oven, the milk should separate in 24 to 30 hours and the curds will come to the top. Stir several times during the process. If milk has not been kept warm enough, it will result in a soft cheese which will settle to the bottom of the bowl. Pour off the whey and reserve for bread making. Put the curds into a colander or strainer lined with dampened cheesecloth; place in refrigerator to drain for several hours. Two quarts of milk will make 2 cups or 1/2 pound of cheese.

MERINGUE CHEESECAKE

FLOUR	2 1/4 cups
SUGAR	1/2 cup
BUTTER	1 cup, softened and cut into pieces
EGG YOLKS	2
COTTAGE CHEESE	1 1/2 cups, sieved
EGG YOLKS	2
LEMON EXTRACT	4 teaspoons
EGG WHITES	4, at room temperature
SUGAR	1/2 cup
FLOUR	2 tablespoons
ALMONDS	6 tablespoons, slivered

For the pastry, put FLOUR and SUGAR in a mixing bowl and work in the BUTTER with finger tips. Add the EGG YOLKS and blend until the dough is smooth. If necessary, add one or two tablespoons more of flour. Roll out into a rectangle and line a jelly roll pan; press some of the dough up the sides to make a half inch rim. Bake in a preheated 350° oven for 15 minutes until half baked. Cool. Turn down oven to 275°. Prepare filling by sieving COTTAGE CHEESE into a bowl. Add EGG YOLKS and LEMON EXTRACT. Beat EGG WHITES until frothy and gradually add SUGAR; beat until glossy. Stir the FLOUR into the cheese mixture and fold in the meringue. Spread the pastry with the cheese mixture. Sprinkle with slivered ALMONDS. Bake in the 275° oven about 40–45 minutes. Let cool and serve at room temperature. Do not refrigerate. Cut into squares. Serves 6.

DESSERT BUTTERMILK FRIES

UNBLEACHED FLOUR	2 cups
SUGAR	1/4 cup
SALT	1 teaspoon
BAKING SODA	1/2 teaspoon
BAKING POWDER	1 teaspoon
NUTMEG	1 teaspoon
BUTTERMILK	3/4 cup
OIL	1/4 cup
EGG	1
OIL	for frying

Combine the first 6 ingredients. Stir in BUTTERMILK and the next 2 ingredients; beat well. Drop from teaspoon into hot OIL, 375°F. Fry until golden; drain. Roll while warm in sugar. Makes about 2 1/2 dozen.

YOGURT

GOAT MILK	or cow milk, 1 quart
CULTURE	1/4 cup plain commercial yogurt at room temperature

Heat MILK to 120°F. or very warm. Cool to a tepid 90°F. and stir the YOGURT into the MILK. Put the liquid into a warm bowl, cover and place in an oven with a pilot light; or place a 4 quart covered pan of boiling water in the oven with the YOGURT bowl. Replenish the boiling water as it cools. This will keep the mixture warm enough to thicken in 6 to 8 hours. It will not be quite as thick as commercial YOGURT. To make another batch reserve 1/4 cup from the last batch. Makes 1 quart YOGURT.

the LaND of MilK aND honey

RIBLAH CHEESE
48 Hour Cheese

SOUR CREAM	1 pint
YOGURT	1 pint
SALT	3/4 teaspoon
ANISE SEED	or caraway, whole, 2 teaspoons
OLIVE OIL	

Mix SOUR CREAM and YOGURT together. Put them in a damp cheesecloth-lined strainer, covering the top with the cheesecloth ends. Place the strainer over a bowl and refrigerate for 36 hours or until mixture is firm; drain liquid and save for bread making. Add SALT and ANISE SEED. Let drain for 12 hours more; drain liquid. Pack cheese into a sterilized jar or crock and refrigerate. It will keep fresh for a week. Serve as an hors d'oeuvre with garlic flavored green olives and Caesarea Thins (p. 80). Makes about 1 pint.

ALMOND CREAM

CREAM	light, 2 cups
MILK	2 cups
CORNSTARCH	1/2 cup
SALT	1/4 teaspoon
SUGAR	2/3 cup
ALMOND EXTRACT	1 teaspoon
MELON BALLS	or any fresh fruit in season

Heat the CREAM and 1 cup of MILK in a double boiler. Mix the CORNSTARCH, SALT and SUGAR with remaining 1 cup MILK and stir until smooth. Combine with the CREAM and MILK mixture and cook over low heat for 20 minutes, stirring constantly, or until thick and smooth. Remove from heat and add ALMOND flavoring; beat until creamy. Pour into a 1 quart mold and chill until firm. Unmold on a round dish and surround with MELON BALLS. Serves 6 to 8.

ALMOND CHEESE DESSERT

CREAMED COTTAGE CHEESE	1/2 pound
SUGAR	1/4 cup
ALMOND EXTRACT	1/4 teaspoon
ALMONDS	1/2 cup, blanched, toasted, chopped
CARDAMOM SEED	ground, 1/4 teaspoon

Beat CHEESE until smooth; add remaining ingredients. Let stand at room temperature for 2 hours. Serve with fruit or cookies. Serves 4.

SOUR CREAM COOKIES

BUTTER	1 cup
SUGAR	1 1/2 cups
EGGS	2
UNBLEACHED FLOUR	or all-purpose, 3 1/2 cups
BAKING SODA	1/2 teaspoon
SALT	1/2 teaspoon
MACE	1 teaspoon
SOUR CREAM	1/4 cup
RAISINS	
NUTS	

Cream BUTTER with SUGAR until well mixed; beat in EGGS one at a time. Add the next 4 ingredients and mix thoroughly; blend in the SOUR CREAM. Drop by teaspoonfuls onto an ungreased baking sheet. Place a RAISIN or NUT in the center of each. Bake in a preheated 350°F. oven for 10 to 12 minutes. Makes about 9 dozen cookies.

PUFF CAKES

BUTTER	1/2 cup
WATER	1 cup
FLOUR	1 cup
EGGS	4
HONEY	or sugar, 1 tablespoon
LEMON EXTRACT	2 teaspoons
OIL	for deep frying

Combine BUTTER and WATER in a saucepan and bring to a boil. Add the FLOUR all at once; remove from heat and stir until the mixture leaves the sides of the pan and forms a ball. Add EGGS, one at a time, and beat vigorously until batter is smooth before adding the next one. Stir in the HONEY and flavoring. Drop by rounded teaspoons into hot OIL, 380°F. If some of the puffs do not turn themselves while cooking, turn with a slotted spoon. Drain on a paper towel; serve with EGGNOG SAUCE (p.184). Makes about 24 puffs.

CREAM PUFFS

BUTTER 1/4 cup
SALT 1/8 teaspoon
WATER 1/2 cup
FLOUR 1/2 cup
EGGS 2

Bring BUTTER, SALT and WATER to a boil in a saucepan; add the FLOUR all at once. Beat until the mixture comes away from the sides of the pan and forms a ball. Remove from heat and add 1 unbeaten EGG at a time, beating until smooth. Drop mixture from a tablespoon onto a greased baking sheet; leave 3 inches between each one. Bake in a preheated 400°F. oven for 20 minutes or until puffed. Turn oven off and leave puffs in oven for 30 minutes or until ready to serve; puffs will be golden and crisp. Makes 6 large puffs or 8 medium ones. Fill with CHEESE PISTACHIO FILLING.

CHEESE PISTACHIO FILLING

RICOTTA CHEESE or creamed cottage cheese, 1 pound
CREAM heavy, 1/2 cup, whipped
PISTACHIO NUTS or walnuts, 1/2 cup, chopped
APRICOT JAM 1/3 cup

Mix the RICOTTA CHEESE and WHIPPED CREAM together and fold in the PISTACHIO NUTS. Slit the sides of

the PUFFS at the base large enough to spoon in the filling.
Melt JAM and spoon over the top of each PUFF. Serves 6.

YOGURT CAKE

BUTTER	1 cup
SUGAR	2 cups
EGGS	4, separated, at room temperature
YOGURT	1 cup
UNBLEACHED FLOUR	or all-purpose, 3 cups
SALT	1/4 teaspoon
BAKING POWDER	4 teaspoons
LEMON EXTRACT	3 teaspoons

Cream the BUTTER and SUGAR together until light and
fluffy. Add the EGG yolks one at a time, beating until
creamy and light. Stir in the YOGURT. Add the FLOUR,
SALT, BAKING POWDER and LEMON EXTRACT; mix
well. Beat the EGG whites until stiff but not dry and mix
1/3 into the batter; fold in the remainder. Turn into a 10
inch tube pan and bake in a preheated 350°F. oven for
about 60 minutes or until cake tester comes out clean. Frost
with Honey Frosting if desired.

HONEY FROSTING

HONEY	1/2 cup
EGG WHITES	2, at room temperature
SALT	1/4 teaspoon
CREAM OF TARTAR	1/8 teaspoon

Bring the HONEY to a boil in a small saucepan. Beat EGG
WHITES until frothy; add SALT and CREAM OF TAR-
TAR, continuing to beat. When EGG WHITES hold soft
peaks, slowly add the HONEY in a thin stream. Continue
to beat until meringue is stiff and glossy.

SOUR CREAM FILLING

SOUR CREAM	1 cup
SUGAR	1/4 cup
FLOUR	1 1/2 tablespoons
EGG YOLK	1, slightly beaten
SALT	1/8 teaspoon
CINNAMON	1/8 teaspoon
NUTMEG	1/8 teaspoon
WALNUTS	1/4 cup, chopped
LEMON EXTRACT	1/2 teaspoon

Heat the SOUR CREAM over low heat. Mix the SUGAR, FLOUR and beaten EGG YOLKS together and slowly stir into the SOUR CREAM. Add the SALT and remaining ingredients. Makes filling for an 8 inch layer cake or a topping for an 8 inch square cake.

ST. JOHN'S CHOCOLATE CAKE

BUTTER	1/2 cup
SUGAR	1 cup
HONEY	3/4 cup
EGGS	2
CAROB POWDER	or cocoa, 1/2 cup
WATER	1/2 cup
UNBLEACHED FLOUR	or all-purpose, 2 1/2 cups
BAKING SODA	1 teaspoon
SALT	1/2 teaspoon
BUTTERMILK	2/3 cup
NUTMEG	freshly grated, 1/2 teaspoon
CINNAMON	ground, 1/2 teaspoon
WALNUTS	chopped, 2/3 cup
HEAVY CREAM	1 cup, whipped
MINT	fresh, chopped, 1 teaspoon or 1/2 teaspoon dried

Cream BUTTER, SUGAR and HONEY. Add EGGS and beat until fluffy. Mix CAROB POWDER with WATER. Stir into creamed mixture and blend well. Combine FLOUR, BAKING SODA, and SALT; add to creamed mixture, alternately with BUTTERMILK, beating after each addition.

Add NUTMEG, CINNAMON and WALNUTS. Bake in an 8 inch greased square pan in a preheated 325° oven for 25 to 30 minutes. Let cool 10 minutes before removing from pan. Continue to cool on a wire rack. Cut into 6 squares. Fold mint into whipped CREAM and put on top. Serves 6.

SCONES OF SEIR

Date Triangles

FLOUR	2 cups
BAKING POWDER	1 tablespoon
SUGAR	2 tablespoons
SALT	1/2 teaspoon
DATES	1/2 cup, pitted and chopped
WALNUTS	1/2 cup, coarsely chopped
EGGS	2
OIL	1/4 cup
LIGHT CREAM	6 tablespoons
SUGAR	

Combine FLOUR, BAKING POWDER, SUGAR and SALT. Add DATES and WALNUTS; toss to coat them thoroughly. Beat 2 EGG yolks and 1 EGG white together and add the OIL and CREAM. Add to the dry ingredients and mix with a fork. Turn out on a floured board and knead a dozen turns. Divide dough in half. Roll into a circle and cut into triangles, 8 to a circle. Brush tops with the other EGG white, slightly beaten, and sprinkle with a little SUGAR. Bake on an ungreased baking sheet in a preheated 400°F. oven for 10 to 12 minutes. Makes 16 scones.

SOUFFLE OF RACHEL

Dessert Pancake

EGGS	2
SALT	1/2 teaspoon
SUGAR	1 teaspoon
FLOUR	1/2 cup
MILK	1/2 cup
BUTTER	3 tablespoons
HONEY SAUCE	
CREAM	heavy, 1/2 pint, whipped, optional

Beat the EGGS and the next 4 ingredients together until well blended. Heat 1 tablespoon BUTTER in a 9 inch skillet, with a heat-proof handle, until BUTTER and pan are very hot; remove from heat and pour in the batter. Immediately place in a preheated 450°F. oven and bake for 5 minutes; reduce heat to 375°F. and bake until it rises unevenly and is golden brown, about 10 to 15 minutes. Serve from the skillet cutting it into wedges. Spoon HONEY SYRUP over each serving and top with whipped CREAM if desired. Serves 6.

CHOCOLATE BREAD PUDDING

CAROB POWDER	or cocoa, 1/2 cup
WATER	6 tablespoons
MILK	3 cups
SUGAR	1/2 cup
SALT	1/8 teaspoon
EGGS	2
CINNAMON	1/2 teaspoon
BREAD CRUMBS	2 cups, day old, torn into very small pieces

Sift CAROB POWDER and mix with WATER; stir until smooth and add MILK. Beat SUGAR, SALT, EGGS and CINNAMON together. Pour CAROB mixture into EGG mixture and blend well. Place BREAD CRUMBS in a 1 1/2 quart greased casserole and pour the combined mixtures over the BREAD CRUMBS. Stir and let stand 20 minutes to absorb liquid. Stir again and place casserole in a pan containing 1 inch of hot water. Bake in a preheated 350°F. oven for about 50 minutes or until a knife inserted in the PUDDING comes out clean. Serves 6.

ST. JOHN'S CHOCOLATE FROSTING

CAROB POWDER	or cocoa, 1 tablespoon
SUGAR	1 cup
MILK	1/3 cup
BUTTER	2 tablespoons
ALMOND EXTRACT	1/4 teaspoon

Mix the first 3 ingredients in a saucepan and cook over medium heat to soft ball stage when tested in cold water. Remove from heat and add BUTTER and ALMOND EX-TRACT; cool to lukewarm and beat until thick. Makes about 1 cup.

CHOCOLATE FISH

BUTTER	soft, 1 cup
SUGAR	1/2 cup
EGG	1
ALMOND EXTRACT	1 1/2 teaspoons
FLOUR	3 cups
BAKING POWDER	1/2 teaspoon
CAROB POWDER	or cocoa, 1/2 cup

Cream BUTTER and SUGAR; beat in EGG. Stir in the remaining ingredients gradually, beating well after each addition. On a lightly floured board roll out the dough 1/8 inch thick and lay the cardboard fish pattern on the dough. Cut around pattern and transfer fish to a greased baking sheet. Press in a piece of raisin or nut for an eye. Bake in the middle of a preheated 300°F. oven for 5 minutes. Remove fish to a rack to cool. Makes about 24 fish.
Note: The cardboard fish pattern is made by drawing a 4 1/2 by 1 1/2 inch oval shape with a triangle attached for a tail.

CHOCOLATE SQUARES

OIL	1/2 cup
CAROB POWDER	or cocoa, 1/2 cup
DATE SUGAR	or white, 1/3 cup
HONEY	1/3 cup

the LaND of MiLk aND honey

EGG	1
MILK	3 tablespoons
UNBLEACHED FLOUR	or all-purpose, 2/3 cup
BAKING POWDER	1 teaspoon
CORIANDER SEED	ground, 1/2 teaspoon
CINNAMON	1/2 teaspoon
WALNUTS	1 cup, chopped

Cream together OIL, CAROB POWDER, DATE SUGAR and HONEY. Stir in the EGG and MILK; beat well. Mix FLOUR, BAKING POWDER, CORIANDER and CINNAMON together. Add the WALNUTS to the FLOUR mixture and toss to coat well. Stir the dry ingredients into the first mixture; beat well and pour into a greased and floured 8 inch square pan. Bake in a preheated 350°F. oven about 25 minutes until cake tester comes out clean. Cut into 16 pieces before cake has cooled.

HONEY CAKE FROM EGYPT

BUTTER	1/4 cup
SUGAR	1/4 cup
HONEY	1/4 cup
EGGS	4, separated, at room temperature
FLOUR	1 1/2 cups
BAKING POWDER	1 teaspoon
CINNAMON	1 teaspoon
WALNUTS	2 1/4 cups, chopped
HONEY CINNAMON SYRUP	

Cream the BUTTER, SUGAR and HONEY together. Add EGG YOLKS and beat until mixture is thick and lemon colored. Beat EGG WHITES until stiff and fold into the egg yolk batter. Combine FLOUR, BAKING POWDER and CINNAMON in a bowl. Add 2 cups of WALNUTS and toss to coat well. Combine the two mixtures, folding in the FLOUR and WALNUTS gently until just blended. Turn into a greased 9 inch square pan and sprinkle with the remaining 1/4 cup WALNUTS. Bake in a preheated 350°F. oven for about 30 minutes or until cake tests done. While still in the pan, cut into diamond shaped pieces and pour over HONEY CINNAMON SYRUP. Let stand several hours before serving.

HONEY CINNAMON SYRUP

HONEY	1 cup
WATER	1/2 cup
CINNAMON	1/2 teaspoon

Combine ingredients and simmer, uncovered, for 10 minutes; cool.

MARY'S KISSES

EGG WHITES	3, at room temperature
SUGAR	1 cup
SALT	1/8 teaspoon
ALMOND EXTRACT	1 teaspoon
CAROB POWDER	or cocoa, 3 tablespoons
WALNUTS	3/4 cup, finely chopped

Beat EGG WHITES with SALT until frothy; very slowly sprinkle in SUGAR, a tablespoonful at a time. Continue to beat until EGG WHITES will stand in peaks. If SUGAR is added too rapidly the meringues will be grainy. Fold in ALMOND EXTRACT, CAROB POWDER and WAL-NUTS. Drop by teaspoonfuls onto ungreased brown paper on a baking sheet. Bake in a preheated 250°F. oven for 30 minutes. Loosen from paper with a spatula. Makes about 40 kisses.

ZIPPORAH'S MERINGUE-TOPPED BREAD PUDDING

EGGS	2, beaten
EGG YOLKS	2, beaten
SUGAR	3/4 cup
SALT	1/4 teaspoon
ALMOND EXTRACT	1/2 teaspoon
BUTTER	3 tablespoons, melted

che LANO OF MiLK ANO hONEY

MILK	1 quart, scalded
BREAD CRUMBS	day old, 2 cups, torn into very small pieces
JAM	6 tablespoons
EGG WHITES	2, at room temperature

Combine EGGS, EGG YOLKS, 1/2 cup SUGAR, SALT, ALMOND EXTRACT and BUTTER; add MILK and blend. Pour over BREAD CRUMBS in a 1 1/2 quart greased casserole. Let stand 20 minutes to soak up custard mixture; stir. Place in a pan of hot water 1 inch deep. Bake in a preheated 350°F. oven for about 1 1/4 hours or until a knife inserted in the center comes out clean. Remove from oven. Spread JAM over hot pudding. Beat EGG WHITES until foamy; beat in remaining 1/4 cup SUGAR and continue to beat until meringue stands in stiff peaks. Cover pudding with meringue; bake 10 minutes or until meringue is golden. Serves 6.

CAROB SWEETS

CAROB POWDER	or cocoa, 6 tablespoons, sifted
SUGAR	1 1/2 cups
CREAM	light, 1/2 cup
BUTTER	soft, 1 tablespoon
ALMOND EXTRACT	1/4 teaspoon

Mix the CAROB POWDER and 1/4 cup water together in a cup. Put SUGAR and CREAM in a saucepan and stir in the CAROB POWDER and water mixture. Cook over medium heat until the mixture reaches the soft ball stage (when a few drops of the mixture forms a soft ball in cold water and can be picked up) or 235°F. on a candy thermometer. While cooking, stir occasionally to keep from sticking. Remove from heat. When bottom of the pan feels cool to the hand, beat in BUTTER and ALMOND EXTRACT. Continue to beat until it begins to lose its shine. Spread in a buttered 8 X 8 X 2 inch pan; cut into pieces and cool thoroughly. One cup of walnuts may be added if desired. Makes 1 pound.

SEED SNAPS

BUTTER	3/4 cup
SUGAR	2/3 cup
EGG	1
UNBLEACHED FLOUR	or all-purpose, 2 cups
BAKING SODA	1/8 teaspoon
SALT	1/8 teaspoon
FENNEL SEED	or anise seed, 2 teaspoons, ground

Cream BUTTER and SUGAR; beat in EGG. Combine FLOUR, BAKING SODA, SALT and FENNEL SEED; gradually stir into first mixture. Mix well; chill for easier handling. Roll out dough on a lightly floured board to 1/16 inch thickness. Cut with a 4 inch cookie cutter. Bake on an ungreased baking sheet in a preheated 400°F. oven for 5 to 6 minutes. Makes about 2 1/2 dozen cookies.

APRICOT TARTS

CREAM CHEESE	6 ounces
BUTTER	1 cup
FLOUR	2 cups
APRICOTS	dried, 12 ounces
SUGAR	1/2 cup

Blend CREAM CHEESE, BUTTER and FLOUR together; chill. Soak APRICOTS 1 hour in water to cover. Add SUGAR and cook, over low heat, until tender; drain well on paper towel and cool. Roll pastry 1/8 inch thick; cut into 2 inch rounds with a cookie cutter. Place half the rounds on an ungreased baking sheet. Place an APRICOT on top of each round; dampen edges and cover with another pastry round; seal edges. Bake in a preheated 375°F. oven for about 6 to 8 minutes. Makes 3 1/2 dozen.

PISTACHIO COOKIES

FLOUR	2 1/2 cups
SUGAR	1 1/2 cups
BAKING POWDER	1 teaspoon
NUTMEG	1/2 teaspoon
BUTTER	1 cup
EGG	1, beaten
WATER	1 tablespoon
ALMOND EXTRACT	1/2 teaspoon
PISTACHIO NUTS	or almonds

Mix the first 4 ingredients together in a bowl. Cut in the BUTTER and mix in the remaining ingredients except the PISTACHIO NUTS. Shape into 1 inch balls and place on a baking sheet. Flatten balls to 1/4 inch thickness. Press 1 or 2 PISTACHIO NUTS in the center of each. Bake in a preheated 350°F. oven about 5 to 6 minutes. Makes 6 1/2 dozen.

NEGEV SAND COOKIES

FLOUR	2 cups
NUTMEG	ground, 1/2 teaspoon
CINNAMON	1/2 teaspoon
DATE SUGAR	or white, 1 cup
BUTTER	2/3 cup
EGG	1, lightly beaten
MILK	1 tablespoon

Mix the first 4 ingredients together. Cut BUTTER into the mixture until it resembles coarse meal. Add EGG and MILK and mix well. Turn out onto a lightly floured board; roll to 1/16 inch thickness. Cut with a 2 inch cookie cutter and place on an ungreased cookie sheet. Bake in a preheated 350°F. oven about 5 to 6 minutes. Do not overbake. Cool on wire racks. Makes about 4 dozen cookies.

JAM GEMS

BUTTER	1/2 cup
SUGAR	1/3 cup
EGG	1, separated
ALMOND EXTRACT	1/4 teaspoon
UNBLEACHED FLOUR	1 cup
SALT	1/2 teaspoon
PISTACHIO NUTS	or walnuts, chopped
JAM	1/2 cup

Cream BUTTER and SUGAR until fluffy; add EGG yolk and flavoring. Stir in FLOUR and SALT. Form into 36 small balls, 1/2 tablespoon of dough for each. Dip in slightly beaten EGG white; roll in nuts. Place on greased baking sheets; make a depression in center of each cookie with fingertip. Bake in a preheated 300°F. for about 15 minutes. While warm fill center with JAM.

CAROB DROPS

BUTTER	1/2 cup
SUGAR	3/4 cup
EGG	1
FLOUR	1 1/8 cups
CAROB POWDER	or cocoa, 3 tablespoons
BAKING POWDER	1/2 teaspoon
BAKING SODA	1/4 teaspoon
SALT	1/8 teaspoon
ALMOND EXTRACT	1/4 teaspoon
WALNUTS	1/2 cup, chopped
RAISINS	1/2 cup

Cream BUTTER and SUGAR; add EGG and beat well. Stir in sifted dry ingredients. Mix in ALMOND EXTRACT, WALNUTS and RAISINS. Drop by well rounded tea-spoonfuls onto an ungreased baking sheet. Bake in a pre-heated 350°F. oven for 6 to 8 minutes. Makes about 24.

the Land of Milk and honey

HONEYED NUTS

NUTS   whole almonds, walnuts and pistachios, 1 cup
SUGAR   1/2 cup
HONEY   1 tablespoon

Toast the NUTS in a 350°F. oven for 10 to 15 minutes. Heat the SUGAR in a saucepan, over low heat, until it melts and begins to caramelize. Blend in the HONEY and stir in the NUTS. Drop onto a greased baking sheet in clusters. Makes about 1/2 pound.

RAMOTH MARINATED CHEESE

ONIONS	1/2 cup, chopped
GARLIC	2 cloves, finely chopped
SALT	1/2 teaspoon
FENNEL SEED	or caraway seed, 1/2 teaspoon
PARSLEY	1/4 cup, chopped
CHEVRE CHEESE	or Danish Muenster, or Mozzarella, 8 ounces, sliced about 1/2 inch thick
OLIVE OIL	3/4 cup
VINEGAR	1/4 cup
PEPPERCORNS	1/4 teaspoon
BAY LEAF	1, large

Combine the first 5 ingredients. Place a layer of the sliced CHEESE in a crock or covered jar and sprinkle with the ONION mixture. Place a second layer of CHEESE and sprinkle with the ONION mixture; repeat. Combine OIL and VINEGAR and pour over the CHEESE to cover. Add the PEPPERCORNS and BAY LEAF. Cover and refrigerate for 3 to 4 days. Serve with crusty bread and Mediterranean olives.

FRAGRANT SPICE CAKE

FLOUR	1 1/2 cups
SALT	3/4 teaspoon
BAKING POWDER	2 teaspoons
BUTTER	1/3 cup
GINGER	1/2 teaspoon, ground

CINNAMON	1/2 teaspoon, ground
NUTMEG	1/4 teaspoon, ground
SUGAR	1 cup
EGG	1 large
MILK	3/4 cup

Mix the first 3 ingredients together and reserve. Cream BUTTER, spices and SUGAR together; beat in EGG. Add flour-mixture alternately with MILK to the sugar-spice mixture; beat batter 1/2 minute. Turn batter into a well greased and lightly floured 9 × 9 × 2 inch pan. Bake in a preheated 350°F. oven for 30 minutes or until cake tests done.

YOGURT CHEESE WITH NUTS

YOGURT	1 quart
WALNUTS	1/2 cup, chopped
ONIONS	6, green, finely chopped
SALT	

Line a strainer with 2 thicknesses of cheesecloth and spoon in the YOGURT. Place strainer in a bowl and chill, letting it drip for 24 hours; discard liquid. Mix in WALNUTS and ONIONS; SALT to taste. Serve as an appetizer with dark bread. Makes about 2 cups.

Note: Onions may be omitted and yogurt cheese may be served with fruit as a dessert.

DESSERT CREAM

CREAM   heavy, 1 cup
BUTTERMILK 1/3 cup

Whip CREAM until stiff. Stir in BUTTERMILK; cover and let stand overnight at room temperature. Serve with any fresh fruit for dessert or as a topping for cakes and puddings.

ROSE AND HONEY SYRUP

HONEY   1/2 cup
SUGAR   3/4 cup
WATER   3 tablespoons
ROSE WATER 2 tablespoons or 1/4 teaspoon almond extract

In a saucepan heat HONEY, SUGAR and WATER together over low heat; stir to dissolve. Simmer 3 minutes or until syrup coats the back of the spoon. Remove from heat and stir in flavoring. Makes about 1 1/2 cups.

POTS OF CREAM

CREAM   medium, 2 cups
SUGAR   1/2 cup
EGG YOLKS   6
ROSE WATER 2 tablespoons
CREAM   heavy, 1/2 cup, whipped, optional

Scald CREAM with SUGAR and cool slightly. Beat EGG YOLKS until thickened. Add the CREAM and SUGAR gradually. Add ROSE WATER. Pour into 6 individual cups and place them in a pan of hot water. Cover tops with foil and bake in a pre-heated 350°F. oven until a knife inserted in the center comes out clean. Serve chilled. Top with whipped CREAM if desired.

Fish of the sea

These shall ye eat of all that are in the waters: whatsoever hath fins and scales in the waters, in the seas, and in the rivers, them shall ye eat.

LEVITICUS 11:9

The waters of the Holy Land teemed with "fins and scales," offering a rich harvest of food and fulfilling God's promise in Genesis that man shall have "dominion over the fish of the sea" (Genesis 1:26). Yet nowhere in the Bible is any special kind of fish mentioned. We are not even sure of the variety of "great fish" that swallowed Jonah.

The only native fish banned from the Hebrews' diet as "unclean" because they lacked "fins and scales" were catfish, eels, lampreys, sharks and skates. However, it is thought that in times of necessity all fish eaten by Christians were eaten by the Hebrews as well.

Since the Sea of Galilee alone offered scores of different fish, from perch and carp to sardines and anchovies, all approved for eating in the Bible, there was no lack of variety. And the Talmud mentions by name many fish familiar to us today, such as salmon, mackeral, tunny (tuna), herring, mullet and swordfish. All were harvested from the rivers and oceans in Old and New Testament times.

Whether boiled, broiled or grilled on open charcoal fires built right on the seashore, or roasted on spits, fish was one of the most popular and plentiful foods available. Sardines and mullet, for in-

Fish of the Sea

stance, were surface fish, and very easy to catch, even with small hand nets. While the Israelites were poor and in bondage in Egypt, these fish were probably one of the few foods they could enjoy in abundance.

But fishing was also the sport of kings, who used first bone and later, in King Solomon's time, iron hooks. From ancient tomb reliefs we have learned that our fishing rod was unknown, and in Bible times fish were caught with hooks, spread nets, spears and even harpoons.

Since the average temperature of the Nile's waters is quite warm, all manner of fish thrived there. Fishing in the Mediterranean was poor in comparison. Perhaps it was fish from the Nile that the Hebrews wept for when they cried out to Moses, "We remember the fish, which we did eat in Egypt freely" (Numbers 11:5).

After they entered the Promised Land, with Jerusalem miles away from the nearest sea coast, the fish which the Hebrews were so fond of were not so easily available. Most of their fish was imported from the Phoenicians or the Philistines, salted, smoked or sun dried and then carried overland where they were sold in fish markets right by the famous Fish Gate of Jerusalem. Merchants did a brisk business even on the Sabbath, according to the prophet Nehemiah:

> There dwelt men of Tyre also therein, which brought fish, and all manner of ware, and sold on the Sabbath unto the children of Judah, and in Jerusalem.
>
> Nehemiah 13:16

In the days of Herod, there was a town called Tarichaea, which was the center of a huge, bustling fish preserving industry. Here, fish were pickled, seasoned and salted before being exported for sale to inland city and town dwellers.

The clear waters of the Sea of Galilee were another popular fishing ground, described by the Jewish historian Josephus in New Testament days: "the sea has fresh water that is very pleasant to drink; the water flows freely and is not muddy."

As the scenes of the Bible shift from Jerusalem to the shores of Galilee, fish appear again and again in the miracles and words of Christ. It was in Galilee, flanked on the west by bare and rocky hills, and to the north by the snow-capped Mount Hermon, that Jesus launched his ministry. Seven of Christ's disciples were fishermen, and the catching and eating of fish is described more frequently in the new Testament than in the Old, especially in the wonderful miracle of the Loaves and Fishes (Mark 6:41, 42).

Frogs, though considered unclean, were probably also eaten at times. Since they proliferated along the banks of the Nile, cooking succulent frogs' legs would have been one way of reducing their numbers during the plague of frogs: "And the rivers shall bring forth frogs abundantly, which shall go . . . into thine ovens and into thy kneading troughs" (Exodus 8:3).

In the New Testament days especially, fish not only played an important role in the diet of the multitudes, but it was chosen to be one of the earliest of all Christian symbols. The first Christians, who did not dare to publicly admit their faith, recognized one another by marking a fish as a secret emblem of their beliefs. The name of Jesus was represented in the form of a fish, since the first five letters of the word "fish" in Greek stood for the initial letters of the five words stating their belief: "Jesus Christ, God's Son, Savior."

BAKED WHITEFISH OF MALTA

BREAD CUBES	3 cups, 1/2 inch cubes
BUTTER	melted, 1/4 cup
CUCUMBER	3/4 cup, chopped
ONION	1/4 cup, chopped
WATER	3 tablespoons
SALT	1/2 teaspoon
PEPPER	freshly ground, 1/8 teaspoon
WHITEFISH	about 3 pounds, cleaned and boned
OIL	

Combine the first 7 ingredients and toss to mix well. Place stuffing lightly in the fish cavity; leave unskewered. Place WHITEFISH in a greased baking pan; brush with OIL. Bake in a preheated 375°F. oven for about 30 minutes or until fish flakes easily. Baste occasionally with OIL. Serves 6.

BAKED STUFFED FISH TIGRAS

WATERCRESS AND RADISH STUFFING

ONION	1/4 cup, chopped
RADISH	1/4 cup, chopped
BUTTER	3 1/2 tablespoons
WATERCRESS	3/4 cup, finely chopped, leaves and stems
SALT	1/4 teaspoon
PEPPER	freshly ground white, 1/8 teaspoon
BREAD CRUMBS	soft, 2 cups
WATER	

Cook ONION and RADISH in BUTTER for 5 minutes. Add WATERCRESS, SALT and PEPPER; mix in BREAD CRUMBS, moisten with WATER and toss well.

BAKED FISH

HADDOCK	or cod, two 1 pound fillets
GARLIC	1 large clove, crushed
SALT	
PEPPER	freshly ground white
BUTTER	1 1/2 tablespoons
CLAM JUICE	1/2 cup
PARSLEY	

Wipe fillets with a damp paper towel. Rub both sides of fillets with GARLIC, SALT and PEPPER. Place 1 fillet in a greased baking pan and spread stuffing to cover. Place the other fillet on top; hold in place with 2 or 3 skewers. Dot top of fillet with BUTTER. Pour in CLAM JUICE and place in a preheated 375°F. oven. Baste several times during the cooking. Bake 20 to 30 minutes or until fish flakes easily. Remove to a warm platter and garnish with PARSLEY. Serves 4 to 6.

BASS GALILEE
Baked Stuffed Bass

OYSTER STUFFING

BUTTER	1/4 cup
ONION	1/4 cup, chopped
TARRAGON	1/4 teaspoon
PARSLEY	1 1/2 tablespoons, chopped
BREAD CRUMBS	2 cups, soft
SALT	
PEPPER	
OYSTERS	1/2 cup, coarsely chopped

Melt BUTTER in a skillet; add ONION and cook 5 minutes.
Add TARRAGON, PARSLEY and BREAD CRUMBS; mix
well. Remove from heat; add SALT and PEPPER to taste.
Lightly mix in the OYSTERS.

BAKED BASS

BASS	3 to 4 pounds, boned, head and tail on, if desired
SALT	
PEPPER	
OYSTER STUFFING	
BACON	
PARSLEY	
RADISHES	

Season BASS lightly with SALT and PEPPER, inside and
out. Fill with OYSTER STUFFING and sew or skewer together. Place several pieces of BACON over fish and bake
in a preheated 350°F. oven for about 35 minutes or until
fish flakes easily. Remove to a heated platter. Garnish with
PARSLEY and RADISHES. Serves 6.

Fish of the sea

CREAMED HADDOCK

SMOKED HADDOCK	(finnan haddie) 1 pound
MILK	2 cups
BUTTER	1/4 cup
SHALLOTS	chopped, 1/4 cup
FLOUR	1/4 cup
MUSTARD	dry, 1 teaspoon
PEPPER	freshly ground, white, 1/8 teaspoon
PARSLEY	2 tablespoons, chopped

Wipe HADDOCK with a damp paper towel and place in a pan just large enough to hold it; pour over the MILK. Bake in a preheated 375°F. oven for 30 minutes. Cook SHALLOTS in BUTTER until tender and golden; stir in FLOUR and MUSTARD. Drain MILK and stir into SHALLOT mixture. Cook until thickened. Flake fish and add to sauce: add PEPPER and PARSLEY. Serve over toast points or turn into a baking dish. Top with bread crumbs and bake until crumbs are brown. Serves 4 to 6.

GRILLED JORDAN TROUT

TROUT	4
SALT	
PEPPER	
BUTTER	1/2 cup, melted
SAVORY LEAVES	fresh, chopped, 1 teaspoon or 1/2 teaspoon dried
ONION	1 tablespoon, grated

Clean and split each fish; leave head and tail on if desired. Allow 1 medium size TROUT per person. Season with SALT and PEPPER. Brush with BUTTER that has been mixed with SAVORY and grated ONION; makes enough to baste 4 TROUT. Place on greased grill bars 6 inches from heat source. Cook 3 minutes on one side, brush with seasoned BUTTER, turn and brush again. Continue to grill until fish flakes when fork tested. Turn only once.

FROGS' LEGS

FROGS' LEGS	18 pairs
SALT	
PEPPER	
FLOUR	
EGGS	2, lightly beaten
WATER	2 tablespoons
BREAD CRUMBS	dry
OIL	
BUTTER	3 tablespoons
GARLIC	2 teaspoons, chopped
PARSLEY	2 tablespoons, chopped

Sprinkle FROGS' LEGS with SALT and PEPPER and coat with FLOUR. Dip them in EGG that has been mixed with the WATER and then into BREAD CRUMBS. In a large skillet, fry the FROGS' LEGS in 1/2 inch OIL turning them once until golden; drain on a paper towel. Heat BUTTER and GARLIC in a small saucepan and when nut brown pour over the FROGS' LEGS; sprinkle with PARSLEY and serve immediately. Serves 6.

CRISP TIDBITS

FILLET OF SOLE	2 pounds
EGG YOLK	1
MILK	1/2 cup
SALT	1/4 teaspoon
PEPPER	1/8 teaspoon, freshly ground
BREAD CRUMBS	dry, 1 1/2 cups
OIL	
PARSLEY	

Cut FILLET OF SOLE diagonally into 1/2 inch strips. Blend EGG YOLK with MILK; add SALT and PEPPER. Soak fish strips in mixture for 10 minutes. Drain. Roll strips in BREAD CRUMBS.

Fry in hot OIL, 375°F., until golden; drain on paper towel. Arrange on a platter and garnish with PARSLEY. Serve with SARAH'S SAUCE (p. 180). Serves 6.

SHAD ROE NAZARETH

ERECH DRESSING	p. 182, or French dressing
SHAD ROE	2 pairs
SAUCE MELITA	p. 181, optional
PARSLEY	2 tablespoons, chopped

Place ROE in a bowl and pour over 1/2 to 3/4 cup of ERECH DRESSING; marinate for an hour or more. Place on a rack over a pan and broil, 6 inches from the heat, on both sides until browned. Baste several times with ERECH DRESSING. Place on a warm platter and sprinkle with PARSLEY. Serve with SAUCE MELITA if desired. Serves 4.

STUFFED SICILIAN SQUID

ONIONS	1 cup, chopped
GARLIC	1 large clove, chopped
FENNEL BULB	or celery, 1/2 cup, finely chopped
OIL	3/4 cup
OLIVES	black, pitted, 1/2 cup, finely chopped, preferably Greek
BREAD CRUMBS	2 cups, soft
TARRAGON	fresh, chopped, 1/2 teaspoon or 1/4 teaspoon dried
MARJORAM	fresh, chopped, 1/2 teaspoon or 1/4 teaspoon dried
CORIANDER	or parsley, 2 tablespoons, chopped
SALT	
PEPPER	
WATER	1 tablespoon
SQUID	6, about 1/2 pound, cleaned

Cook ONIONS, GARLIC, and FENNEL in 3 tablespoons OIL until tender. Remove from heat and stir in the OLIVES, BREAD CRUMBS, TARRAGON, MARJORAM and CORIANDER. SALT and PEPPER to taste. Moisten with WATER; stuff the SQUID. Heat remaining OIL in a skillet and fry the SQUID about 5 to 6 minutes on each side. Do not salt while cooking since it will toughen them. Serve as an appetizer or entree. Serves 6.

COLD SUMMER PLATTER

SALT	
CUCUMBER	1, peeled, quartered lengthwise, halved
FILLET OF SOLE	4, cut in half lengthwise to make 8 pieces
OIL	2 tablespoons
GARLIC	1 large clove, finely chopped
PEPPER	freshly ground
STOCK	chicken, 1 cup
TARRAGON	fresh, chopped, 1/2 teaspoon or 1/4 teaspoon dried
SAVORY	fresh, chopped, 1/2 teaspoon, or 1/4 teaspoon dried
WATERCRESS	
SOUR CREAM	1 cup
GREEN ONIONS	1/4 cup, finely chopped

Lightly SALT CUCUMBER wedges and FILLETS. Trim FILLETS to make them the same length. Roll FILLET pieces around CUCUMBER wedges; secure with wooden picks. Heat OIL and cook the GARLIC, over low heat without browning, for 1 minute. Add 1/4 teaspoon SALT, PEPPER, STOCK and prepared FILLETS. Cover and cook over low heat about 6 minutes or until fish flakes easily; baste several times with the liquid. Remove to a dish and pour the liquid over. Cover and chill; remove the picks. To serve, arrange FILLETS on a platter in a circle and place WATERCRESS in the center. Top the FILLETS with SOUR CREAM and sprinkle with GREEN ONIONS. Serves 8.

SEA CREATURES
WITH SHELLS

. . . the waters brought forth abundantly.
GENESIS 1:21

Shellfish were rich fruits of the sea treasured and eaten by the people of the Holy Land. The oyster and its rare and costly pearl were well known to the rich. Job compares the priceless wealth of wisdom to that of the pearl when he asks for the gift of understanding: "No mention shall be made of coral, or of pearls; for the price of wisdom is above rubies" (Job 28:18).

While oysters and other sea delicacies such as mussels and shrimp are debatable as food in the Bible, all were probably eaten and enjoyed at one time or another. There were also many species of conch in the Red Sea; in Exodus God instructs Moses to mix the powder of a crushed conch shell with frankincense to prepare a fragrant perfume for His temple.

Snails too were gathered and, when dried and ground, produced a beautiful purple and scarlet dye for robes and hangings. Although considered unclean (Leviticus 11:30), snails were eaten in times of scarcity, as were turtles. Turtle eggs, in fact, were prized as a delicacy by the wealthy of the period.

BROILED CLAMS

HARD SHELL CLAMS	small, 24
BUTTER	1/3 cup
GARLIC	1 teaspoon, finely chopped
PARSLEY	1 tablespoon, finely chopped
TARRAGON	fresh, chopped, 1/2 teaspoon or 1/4 teaspoon dried
THYME	fresh, chopped, 1/2 teaspoon, or 1/4 teaspoon dried
OREGANO	fresh, chopped, 1/2 teaspoon, or 1/4 teaspoon dried
BREAD CRUMBS	fine, dry, 3/4 cup
SALT	
PEPPER	

Open CLAMS or place them in a 450°F. oven just long enough to open, 8 to 10 minutes; reserve CLAM liquid. With a sharp knife loosen the CLAMS from the connecting muscle and place the CLAMS in shells on a broiler pan. Spoon a few drops of the CLAM liquid over each to moisten. Melt BUTTER in a small pan and add GARLIC, PARSLEY and herbs. Cook over low heat for 3 to 4 minutes; add the BREAD CRUMBS and toss lightly; add SALT and PEPPER to taste. Spoon mixture over the CLAMS. Broil 6 inches from heat about 3 minutes or until heated through. Serves 4.

LOBSTER SALAD

LOBSTER	2, about 1 pound each, cooked, split, cleaned
ARTICHOKE BOTTOMS	1 cup, cooked, chopped, or chopped cucumber
EGGS	2, hard-cooked, chopped
FENNEL BULB	or celery, 1/2 cup, chopped
BLACK OLIVES	preferably Greek, rinsed, pitted, chopped, 1/4 cup
GREEN ONIONS	1/4 cup, chopped
JAVAN DRESSING	p. 183, 1/2 cup
SALT	

sea creatures with shells

PEPPER

WATERCRESS   or parsley

Remove meat from LOBSTER body and claws; cut into bite size pieces. Put into a bowl with the next 6 ingredients; add SALT and PEPPER to taste. Fill the 4 LOBSTER half shells with the mixture. Garnish with WATERCRESS. Serves 4. Note: Two cups of crab, salmon or tuna may be substituted for LOBSTER, and served on a bed of lettuce.

GRECIAN CRAB

BUTTER	3 tablespoons
FLOUR	3 tablespoons
MILK	1 cup
SALT	1 teaspoon
PEPPER	white, ground, 1/8 teaspoon
MUSTARD	dry, 3/4 teaspoon
CHIVES	finely chopped, 1 tablespoon
CRABMEAT	picked over to remove bits of shell, 2 cups
BREAD CRUMBS	dry
EGGS	2, beaten
OIL	for frying

Make the cream sauce by mixing the BUTTER, FLOUR, and MILK. Season with SALT, PEPPER, MUSTARD, and CHIVES. Mix CRABMEAT with sauce. Chill 1 hour or more. Shape into about 50 small balls if used as appetizer or 6 to 8 patties if used as a main course. Roll them in BREAD CRUMBS, beaten EGGS, and then in BREAD CRUMBS again. Fry in deep fat at 375° until brown. Serve hot with PARSLEY SAUCE (p. 183).

SHRIMP IN MELON

MUSTARD	dry, 1 teaspoon
CURRY POWDER	1/4 to 1/2 teaspoon
ONION JUICE	1 tablespoon
JAVAN DRESSING	p. 183, or mayonnaise, 1/2 cup
SOUR CREAM	2 tablespoons
CANTALOUPE	1, about 2 1/2 pounds
SHRIMP	large, 1 pound, shelled, deveined, cooked
WATERCRESS	

Mix the first 5 ingredients together. Refrigerate. Slice off one end of the MELON 3 inches down. Scoop out seeds. Remove meat and cut into cubes or use a melon scoop. Remove remainder of uneven meat from melon leaving the shell. When ready to serve, mix the SHRIMP AND MELON cubes with the sauce and fill the shell. Place the top on the MELON and serve surrounded by WATERCRESS. Serves 4.

STUFFED BROILED SHRIMP

STUFFING FOR BROILED SHRIMP

BREAD CRUMBS	soft, fine, 3 cups
PARSLEY	flat, 2 tablespoons, finely chopped
SHALLOTS	2 tablespoons, chopped
GARLIC	1 teaspoon, finely chopped
BUTTER	2 tablespoons
SALT	
PEPPER	

Moisten BREAD CRUMBS with WATER; add PARSLEY and make into a paste. Cook SHALLOTS and GARLIC in butter over low heat for 5 minutes; do not brown. Stir into the paste mixture, with remaining BUTTER in the pan. SALT and PEPPER to taste.

BROILED SHRIMP

SHRIMP	raw, 1 pound, peeled, deveined and split lengthwise almost through
BUTTER	6 tablespoons
GARLIC	1/2 teaspoon, finely minced
PARSLEY	2 tablespoons, finely chopped

Flatten SHRIMP being careful not to disconnect the halves. Place the STUFFING on top of the SHRIMP covering the entire surface. Melt BUTTER in a small saucepan; add GARLIC and PARSLEY and cook 1 minute over low heat. Place SHRIMP in a shallow baking pan and pour over the hot seasoned BUTTER to coat each SHRIMP. Broil 6 inches from source of heat until SHRIMP are pink. Serves 4.

SEA CREATURES WITD SDELLS

BROILED SCALLOPS AND SHRIMPS ON SKEWERS

SCALLOPS	1 pound, thoroughly washed and drained
SHRIMP	1 1/2 pounds, medium size, peeled, deveined
CLAM JUICE	1 cup
GARLIC	1 clove, crushed
BAY LEAF	1, crumbled
PEPPERCORNS	12
ONION	1 medium, sliced
OLIVE OIL	1/3 cup
VINEGAR	tarragon, 1 tablespoon
SALT	1 1/4 teaspoons

Cut SCALLOPS in half if large and place in a bowl with the SHRIMP. Combine remaining ingredients; pour marinade over sea food and cover. Refrigerate several hours. When ready to serve, thread 4 SHRIMP alternately with 4 SCAL-LOPS on each of 6 skewers. Broil 4 inches from heat for 6 to 8 minutes or until lightly browned, turning to cook all sides. Baste with remaining marinade during broiling. Serves 6.

CREAMED OYSTERS

NUTMEG	1/4 teaspoon
GINGER	ground, 1/4 teaspoon
OYSTER LIQUOR	3/4 cup
STOCK	chicken, 1/2 cup
OYSTERS	1 quart
BUTTER	2 tablespoons
FLOUR	3 tablespoons
ALMONDS	blanched, ground, 1/2 cup
SALT	
PEPPER	
TOAST	4 slices
PARSLEY	

Combine in a saucepan NUTMEG, GINGER, OYSTER LI-QUOR and STOCK. Simmer 3 minutes; add the OYS-TERS and cook over low heat until the edges of the OYS-TERS begin to curl. Remove the OYSTERS and keep warm. Strain the liquid through a dampened cheesecloth. In a saucepan melt BUTTER, blend in FLOUR and cook 1 minute. Pour in the strained liquid and cook until thickened. Add the ALMONDS and OYSTERS; heat, and add SALT and PEPPER to taste. Serve on slices of buttered toast. Garnish with PARSLEY. Serves 4.

STUFFED BROILED LOBSTER

LOBSTERS	live, 4, 1 1/4 to 1 1/2 pounds
BREAD CRUMBS	soft, 1 1/3 cups
ALMONDS	3/4 cup, blanched, chopped
BUTTER	3/4 cup
TARRAGON	fresh, chopped, 1 teaspoon or 1/2 teaspoon dried
SALT	1/2 teaspoon
PEPPER	freshly ground, 1/8 teaspoon
MELTED BUTTER	

Split LOBSTERS and crack claws. Remove green tomalley and coral. (The tomalley and coral may be added to the BREAD CRUMBS and ALMONDS, if desired.) Remove and discard dark vein and sac. Prepare stuffing in a skillet by tossing BREAD CRUMBS and ALMONDS in BUTTER over low heat until golden. Add TARRAGON, SALT and PEPPER. Place LOBSTERS on broiling pans, shell side down, and brush with melted BUTTER. Broil 6 inches from heat for 12 to 15 minutes, basting with melted BUTTER frequently. Remove LOBSTERS and fill with stuffing; brush with BUTTER. Place under broiler again long enough to brown lightly. Serve with melted BUTTER. Serves 8.

MUSSELS IN SAUCE

MUSSELS	4 pounds
ONIONS	2, chopped
SHALLOTS	or green onions, 1/2 cup, finely chopped
GARLIC	1 tablespoon, finely chopped

SEA CREATURES WITH SHELLS

BUTTER	3/4 cup
STOCK	chicken, 2 cups
SALT	1 teaspoon
PEPPER	freshly ground, 1/4 teaspoon
PARSLEY	1/4 cup, chopped
VINEGAR	1 teaspoon

Wash and scrub MUSSELS with a stiff brush and remove the black beard. In a large kettle cook the ONIONS, SHALLOTS and GARLIC in 6 tablespoons BUTTER for 5 minutes. Place the scrubbed MUSSELS on top; add the STOCK, SALT, PEPPER and 2 tablespoons each PARSLEY and BUTTER. Cover and steam until shells open, about 5 to 7 minutes. Do not overcook; when shells open they are done. Sprinkle with remaining 2 tablespoons PARSLEY. With a slotted spoon remove the MUSSELS to a soup tureen. Add remaining 1/4 cup BUTTER and the VINEGAR to the sauce. Boil 2 minutes and strain through a damp cheesecloth over the MUSSELS in tureen or serve in individual bowls. Serve with crusty bread. Serves 4.

biRÖs of the aiR

. . . and let fowl multiply in the earth.

GENESIS 1:22

In Deuteronomy the Lord forbids the eating of vultures, eagles, ravens and other birds of prey, but He invites man to enjoy all the clean fowls of the air (Deuteronomy 14:11–18). The savory, plump pigeon, tender quail, tasty and succulent partridge—many of the fowl that Adam, the world's first bird watcher, saw fly overhead—were snared and savored in Bible times, just as they are today. And no wonder. Besides being the home for hundreds of species, the Holy Land was also a stopping off place for many seasonal winged visitors on their way north or south. Almost every type of bird found in Africa, Europe and Asia crosses the Holy Land at some stage of its migratory route.

Even today, the miracle of Moses is repeated each fall and spring, as huge flocks of these bold birds fly their way from Europe across the sea to Africa and western Asia and back again. If the wind shifts while the birds are in flight, they are blown off course, and as in the miracle in the wilderness, they may fall exhausted into the sea or desert sands.

The quail is the bird known to us from the two miracles of Moses in the wilderness. Hungry, tired and fearful after their escape from Egypt, the Israelites wept bitter tears for meat and drink, their cries ringing across the empty desert. "And there went forth a wind from the Lord, and brought quails from the sea, and let them fall by the camp" (Numbers 12:31). Flesh rained as dust, and as many as the sands of the sea were the fowl that fell to the earth, according to Psalm 78:27. These small tasty game birds were stored in straw baskets, cooked in pots, or strung up to dry in the sun.

The sand colored partridges, so enjoyed by the Hebrews, and very abundant, were most often roasted or broiled. These game birds were scattered across the Holy Land, from the Sinai Desert to the rocky hillsides of the rolling Jordan valley.

During the time of plenty, "Solomon's provision for one day was thirty measures of fine flour, and three-score measures of meal, ten fat oxen, and twenty oxen out of the pastures, and an hundred sheep, besides harts, and roebucks and fallow deer, and fatted fowl" (I Kings 4:22–23). The "fatted fowl" served at the groaning tables of Solomon's feasts were most likely geese. Descended from the Asian jungle fowl, these game birds were known in Israel more than six hundred years before Christ. Along with the ducks which floated in the swamps of bulrushes and papyrus, or in the Sea of Galilee, geese are referred to often in both the Old and New Testament, and are thought to be the first birds domesticated by man.

If geese graced the tables of rich and poor alike in Bible times, the meat of the peacock was a luxury reserved for only the wealthy. Phoenician traders brought the first peacocks from India to the court of the Pharoahs while the Hebrews still toiled at the Pyramids, but the bird was unknown to the Israelites until the time of Solomon. "For the king had at sea a navy of Tharshish, with the navy of Hiram: once in three years came the navy of Tharshish, bringing gold, and silver, ivory, and apes, and peacocks" (I Kings 10:22). This is the oldest written record of the peacock's history outside of India, and while the royal bird proudly roamed the terraced gardens of Solomon, its green-blue feathers awing even the Queen of Sheba—the peacock was also highly prized as a table bird. Akin to the turkey and the partridge, the peafowl, or peahen, while darker and less colorful than its mate, still provided a delicious departure from everyday dishes.

While the peacock was a delicacy reserved for the court of kings, the humble pigeon was in every courtyard; it is the bird most often found in the pages of the Bible. The dove which brought the olive branch to Noah's ark was an ancestor of our own pavement bound city-dweller, and its gentle cooing could be heard from the roofs of old Palestine, welcoming the spring. "For lo, the winter is past, the rain is over and gone. The flowers appear on the earth, the time of the singing of birds is come, and the voice of the turtle is heard in our land" (The Song of Solomon 2:11–12).

ROAST GOOSE WITH WHEAT PILAF STUFFING

GOOSE	1, 12 to 14 pounds
SALT	
PEPPER	
WHEAT PILAF STUFFING	

Remove as much fat from inside of bird as possible. Rub inside and out with SALT and PEPPER. Fill the cavities with WHEAT PILAF STUFFING and skewer together. Place in baking pan on rack in a preheated 325°F. oven and roast for about 4 1/2 hours. Prick skin every half hour; pour off fat as it accumulates. Test for doneness by moving drumsticks, which should move easily when done. Pour off all but 4 tablespoons of fat and make gravy with 4 table-spoons flour and 2 cups of stock made from cooking neck and giblets in salted water. Serves 8.

WHEAT PILAF STUFFING

GREEN ONIONS	3/4 cup, chopped
BUTTER	1/2 cup
CRACKED WHEAT	3 cups
STOCK	chicken, 6 cups
SALT	1 1/2 teaspoons
PEPPER	1/4 teaspoon, freshly ground
THYME	fresh, chopped, 1 1/2 teaspoons or 3/4 teaspoon dried

MARJORAM	fresh, chopped, 1 1/2 teaspoons, or 3/4 teaspoon dried
RAISINS	golden, 3/4 cup
WALNUTS	or almonds, 1/2 cup, chopped

Cook ONIONS in BUTTER for 5 minutes; add CRACKED WHEAT and cook over medium heat for 5 minutes, stirring continually. Add the STOCK and the next 3 ingredients. Cover and simmer 20 to 30 minutes until water is absorbed. Remove from heat and add RAISINS and NUTS. Cool before stuffing.

GOOSE WITH GRAPE STUFFING

ONION	1 1/2 cups, finely chopped
FENNEL BULB	or celery, 1 cup, finely chopped
BUTTER	1/2 cup
GRAPE JUICE	6 tablespoons
GRAPE JELLY	or jam, 1/4 cup
SALT	1/2 teaspoon
SAGE	1 teaspoon
MARJORAM	1 1/2 teaspoons
THYME	1 1/2 teaspoons
BREAD CRUMBS	coarse, dry, 6 cups
PISTACHIO NUTS	or almonds, 1/2 cup, chopped
GOOSE	1, 12 to 14 pounds

In a skillet cook ONIONS and FENNEL in BUTTER over low heat until tender but not brown. Add GRAPE JUICE and JELLY; remove from heat when JELLY is melted. Add the remaining ingredients and toss lightly. Cool before stuffing the goose.
Note: See Roast Goose with Wheat Pilaf Stuffing for directions on preparing the goose.

135

DUCK PHENICIA
Roast Duck With Walnut Dressing

DUCK	4 to 5 pounds, ready to cook
BREAD CUBES	4 cups firm white or whole wheat, 2 days old, cut into 1/4 inch cubes
EGGS	2, hard-cooked, chopped coarsely
RAISINS	2 tablespoons
CORIANDER LEAVES	1 tablespoon fresh, chopped or 1/2 tablespoon dried
HONEY	1 tablespoon
WATER	3 tablespoons
OIL	3 tablespoons
ONIONS	1 cup, chopped
GARLIC	1 tablespoon, chopped
CUMIN SEED	1/4 teaspoon, ground
CORIANDER SEED	1/4 teaspoon, ground
ANISE SEED	1/4 teaspoon, ground
RADISHES	1 cup, chopped, red or white
WALNUTS	1/2 cup, chopped
SALT	
PEPPER	

Wash the DUCK under cold running water and pat dry inside and out with paper towels. Combine BREAD CUBES and the next 5 ingredients in a bowl and toss lightly. In a heavy skillet heat the OIL and cook the ONION and GARLIC until golden. Add the remaining ingredients and cook 3 minutes longer. Spoon the contents of the skillet over the bread mixture and toss thoroughly; SALT and PEPPER to taste. Put dressing loosely into each of the cavities and sew or skewer the openings securely. Prick the skin of the DUCK all over with a skewer at inch intervals. Truss the DUCK and place it on its side on a rack in a shallow pan. Roast in a preheated 325°F. oven for 1/2 hour, turn the DUCK onto its other side and roast 1/2 hour longer. Turn the DUCK breast side up and roast for 1 1/2 hours basting occasionally with the fat. To test for doneness, pierce the thigh of the DUCK with the point of a sharp knife. If the juice is still slightly pink, continue roasting for another 15 minutes or until done. Let the DUCK rest for 10 minutes for easier carving. Serves 4.

bircs of the air

AHASUERUS' FAVORITE DUCK

OIL	olive, 2 tablespoons
DUCK	1, about 5 pounds, cut into 8 serving pieces
ONIONS	2 medium, chopped
TUMERIC	1/2 teaspoon
FENNEL SEED	ground, 1/4 teaspoon
FLOUR	2 tablespoons
WALNUTS	1 cup, chopped
POMEGRANATE JUICE	1 1/2 cups juice and 1 1/2 cups water, or 3 cups cranberry juice
SALT	1 1/2 teaspoons
PEPPER	1/8 teaspoon

Heat OIL in skillet and brown DUCK pieces on all sides; remove to paper towel. Drain off all but 2 tablespoons of the fat and cook ONIONS 5 minutes. Stir in TUMERIC, FENNEL SEED and FLOUR and cook 1 minute more. Return DUCK pieces to skillet and add remaining ingredients. Cover and simmer 1 1/2 hours, turning pieces twice during cooking; correct seasoning. Arrange pieces in serving dish. Remove any fat which rises to the top of the sauce; serve sauce in a bowl. Serves 4.

SPIT-ROASTED WILD DUCKS

WILD DUCKS
SALT
PEPPER
ONIONS
FENNEL TOPS
BACON
STOCK   made from duck giblets

Pluck, singe and clean each bird; wash inside and out and pat dry. Season with SALT and PEPPER. Place 1 ONION and a few FENNEL TOPS in each cavity and skewer; wrap in BACON and secure with metal picks. Place on spit 6 inches from source of heat. Baste with STOCK as birds turn. Cook 12 to 20 minutes depending on size of birds.

When done, remove contents from cavities and discard along with the BACON. Wild duck flesh is done when it is pink.

DUCK SALAMIS

DUCK	4 pound
SALT	
PEPPER	
SHILOH STUFFING	p. 179
STOCK	from boiling neck and giblets, 2 cups
DATE SUGAR	or brown, 1/2 cups
CLOVES	ground, 1/16 teaspoon
MUSTARD	dry, 1 teaspoon

Season the cavity with SALT and PEPPER. Stuff with SHILOH STUFFING; skewer. Roast uncovered about 2 hours or until done in a preheated 325°F. oven. Baste every 30 minutes with STOCK and the remaining ingredients mixed together. Serves 4.

PARTRIDGE IN A SKILLET

SALT	
PEPPER	
PARTRIDGES	3, cleaned, ready to cook, or Rock Cornish
GARLIC	1 large clove, crushed
JUNIPER BERRIES	16, crushed
BACON	6 slices
BUTTER	clarified, 1/4 cup
OREGANO LEAVES	fresh, 4 whole, bruised or 1 teaspoon dried
OLIVES	18 green, pitted
STOCK	from partridge giblets, 1 cup
WATERCRESS	

SALT and PEPPER the PARTRIDGES and rub inside and out with GARLIC. Place JUNIPER BERRIES inside each cavity and skewer. Wrap BACON around each bird and secure with metal picks. Place BUTTER in a large skillet and when hot add the PARTRIDGES; brown evenly turning on all sides. Add OREGANO LEAVES and OLIVES; pour in the STOCK and simmer 45 minutes, basting occasionally, until done. Arrange birds on a warm platter and garnish with cooked OLIVES and WATERCRESS. Serves 6.

SPIT-ROASTED PHEASANT

PHEASANT
QUINCE   or apple slices
FENNEL BULB   or celery slices
BUTTER
STOCK   made from cooking giblets

Pluck, singe and clean bird. Wash inside and out and pat dry. Put slices of QUINCE and FENNEL BULB into the cavity and skewer. Place on spit 8 inches from source of heat. Baste frequently with a mixture of half melted BUTTER and half STOCK. Cook until the juices no longer run pink when a fork penetrates deeply into the flesh, about 1 hour. One PHEASANT serves 2 to 3 people.

BROILED QUAIL FOR DESERT WANDERERS

QUAIL   4, or Rock Cornish
BUTTER   1/4 cup, melted
SALT
PEPPER
GRAPE JUICE   1/4 cup
PARSLEY   2 tablespoons, finely chopped

Pluck, singe and clean each bird; split in half. Brush with BUTTER and sprinkle with SALT and PEPPER. Grill on a well greased rack, starting with split side down, turning once and finishing on skin side. Grill 8 to 10 minutes on each side about 6 inches from the heat. Mix together 1/4 cup melted BUTTER, GRAPE JUICE, and PARSLEY to pour over the QUAIL before serving.

biRÒs of
the couRtYARÒ

. . . and the cock crew.
MARK 14:68

The crowing of the cock is even less welcome after its significance in
the New Testament. Its call at dawn signalled that Christ's disciple
Peter had denied him thrice. This biblical cock differs little from our
familiar farmyard variety. Easily the most valuable bird in the world,
it descends from the red jungle fowl that King Solomon's navy may
have brought from as far away as India, Burma, and Malaya. At that
time the eggs of all fowl were highly prized and enjoyed as great
delicacies.

Chickens were probably domesticated more than five thousand
years ago in India for the sport of cock fighting. Gradually losing
their power to fly, the birds were not raised for food until several
hundred years before Christ's birth. Then they were kept in courtyards for convenience. It is interesting to note that no new type of
fowl, with the exception of the Rock Cornish, has been developed
over the years.

Christ Himself makes the only literal reference to the fowl in the
Bible when he laments the blindness of Jerusalem to its prophets:
"How often would I have gathered thy children together, even as a
hen gathereth her chickens under her wings, and ye would not!"
(Matthew 23:37).

140

CHICKEN IN SOUR CREAM

CHICKEN	1 broiler or fryer, 2 1/2 to 3 1/2 pounds, cut into serving pieces
OIL	3 tablespoons
GARLIC	1 clove, minced
ONION	3 tablespoons, chopped
FLOUR	2 tablespoons
SALT	1 teaspoon
PEPPER	1/4 teaspoon, freshly ground
TARRAGON	fresh, chopped, 1 teaspoon or 1/2 teaspoon dried
CHICKEN STOCK	1 1/2 cups, made from giblets
ALMONDS	toasted and slivered, 1/4 cup
SOUR CREAM	3/4 cup, at room temperature
ROMANO CHEESE	grated, 2 tablespoons

In a skillet brown CHICKEN in OIL; remove. Add GARLIC and ONION and cook until tender, but not brown. Blend in FLOUR, SALT, PEPPER and TARRAGON. Stir in STOCK. Cook, stirring constantly, until mixture is smooth and thickened. Return CHICKEN to skillet; sprinkle with a few ALMONDS. Cover and cook over low heat for 45 minutes or until CHICKEN is tender. Remove CHICKEN to a shallow casserole and keep warm. Blend the SOUR CREAM into the sauce. Correct the seasoning and pour over the CHICKEN. Sprinkle with CHEESE and remaining ALMONDS. Serves 4.

BRAISED CHICKEN

CHICKEN	2 1/2 to 3 pounds, cut into serving pieces
OIL	2 or 3 tablespoons
ONIONS	2 large, sliced
GINGER ROOT	fresh, chopped, 2 teaspoons or 1/2 teaspoon ground ginger
CORIANDER	ground, 1/4 teaspoon
CUMIN SEED	ground, 1/4 teaspoon

141

biblical garoen cookery

CINNAMON	ground, 1/8 teaspoon
CLOVES	ground, 1/8 teaspoon
SALT	1 teaspoon
PEPPER	freshly ground white
GARLIC	1 1/2 teaspoons, finely chopped
POMEGRANATE JUICE	1 cup, or water
VINEGAR	tarragon, 1 tablespoon
GRENADINE SYRUP	3 tablespoons or half cranberry juice and half honey

In a large skillet brown CHICKEN in OIL; remove to a plate. Add the ONIONS to the skillet and cook 5 minutes. Return CHICKEN pieces to the skillet. Stir in the spices, SALT, PEPPER and GARLIC. Add POMEGRANATE JUICE, VINEGAR and GRENADINE SYRUP. Cover and simmer over low heat until CHICKEN is tender. Remove CHICKEN to a warm platter. Thicken sauce if desired with a little flour and water. Correct seasoning and pour over CHICKEN. Serves 4.

CHICKEN WITH LAMB STUFFING

BUTTER	6 tablespoons
PINE NUTS	2 tablespoons
LAMB	1 pound, ground
SALT	1 teaspoon
PEPPER	freshly ground black, 1/8 teaspoon
CINNAMON	ground, 1/2 teaspoon
NUTMEG	ground, 1/4 teaspoon
CORIANDER SEED	ground, 1/4 teaspoon
BARLEY	or rice, cooked, 1 cup
ROASTING CHICKEN	about 3 to 4 pounds, ready to cook
OIL	

In a small pan brown PINE NUTS in 1 tablespoon BUTTER; reserve. In a skillet brown LAMB in 5 tablespoons BUTTER; stir in SALT, PEPPER, CINNAMON, NUTMEG and CORIANDER and cook 1 minute more. Remove from heat and stir in PINE NUTS and BARLEY; cool. Stuff body and neck cavity of CHICKEN with LAMB mixture. Sew or skewer openings. Place CHICKEN on a rack in a shallow open pan and brush with OIL. Roast in a preheated 350°F. oven about 2 hours until CHICKEN is tender and well browned. Serves 6.

CHICKEN GAZA

FRYING CHICKENS	2, cut into serving pieces
SALT	
PEPPER	freshly ground
GARLIC	1 large clove, finely chopped
ONIONS	3 medium, thinly sliced
BUTTER	3 tablespoons
STOCK	chicken, 1 cup
SOUR CREAM	2 cups
OLIVES	black, 3/4 cup, pitted, chopped

Season the CHICKEN with SALT and PEPPER. Cook GARLIC and ONIONS in BUTTER over medium heat for 5 minutes; remove from pan. Add the CHICKEN and brown on all sides. Add STOCK and return ONIONS to the pan. Cover and simmer 1 hour or until CHICKEN is tender. Stir in SOUR CREAM and OLIVES. Simmer 10 minutes longer, but do not boil or cream will curdle. Serve with bulgur. Serves 6 to 8.

CHICKEN WITH MINT AND HERB SAUCE

OLIVE OIL	2 tablespoons
GARLIC	2 teaspoons, finely chopped
CUMIN	1/2 teaspoon, ground
CORIANDER	1/4 cup finely chopped fresh leaves or 2 tablespoons dried
MINT	fresh, 1/4 cup finely chopped leaves
CHICKEN BREASTS	4 single
SALT	
PEPPER	freshly ground white
ONION	1 large, thinly sliced
WATER	1 cup

143

Combine OIL, GARLIC, CUMIN, CORIANDER and MINT in a mortar and pestle, or a small bowl, and mix and crush with a wooden spoon. Wipe the CHICKEN BREASTS with a paper towel and sprinkle with SALT and PEPPER. Rub both sides of the BREASTS with the herb paste. Spread ONIONS in a roasting pan; pour in the WATER and place BREASTS on top of the ONIONS. Cover and braise in a preheated 375°F. oven for 30 minutes or until tender. Remove cover and place under broiler until golden. Serve the CHICKEN with the braising sauce. Serves 4.

COURTYARD SALAD
Chicken Walnut Salad

EGGS	3, hard-cooked
CHICKEN	3 cups, cooked, diced
CUCUMBERS	3, peeled, seeds removed, diced
WALNUTS	1/2 cup, chopped
PARSLEY	2 tablespoons, finely chopped
CHIVES	1 tablespoon, finely chopped
JAVAN DRESSING	p. 183, 1 cup
SALT	
PEPPER	
LETTUCE	

Chop the EGG whites and EGG yolks separately. Mix the next 5 ingredients with EGG whites and JAVAN DRESSING; add SALT and PEPPER to taste. Pile the salad in the center of a serving dish; surround with LETTUCE leaves. Sprinkle the top with chopped EGG yolks. Serves 6.

SHUSHAN CHICKEN LOAF

CHICKEN	4 cups, cooked, ground
BREAD CRUMBS	soft, 1 1/2 cups
EGGS	2, slightly beaten
MILK	2/3 cup
STOCK	chicken, 1/3 cup
FENNEL BULB	or celery, 1/3 cup, finely chopped
ONION	1/3 cup, finely chopped

SALT	1 1/4 teaspoons
PEPPER	freshly ground, 1/8 teaspoon
MARJORAM	fresh, chopped, 1/4 teaspoon or 1/8 teaspoon dried
THYME	fresh, chopped, 1/4 teaspoon or 1/8 teaspoon dried
NUTMEG	1/8 teaspoon
PARSLEY	

Combine all ingredients except PARSLEY and mix well; turn into a well greased 8 1/2 × 4 1/2 × 2 1/2 inch loaf pan. Bake in a preheated 350°F. oven for about 45 minutes or until center is firm. Invert onto a warm platter and garnish with PARSLEY. Serves 6.

SQUAB JERUSALEM

ONION	1 medium, finely chopped
BUTTER	
BREAD CRUMBS	stale, 1 cup
HAM	or tongue, 1 cup, chopped
PINE NUTS	1/2 cup
PARSLEY	1/4 cup, chopped
SAVORY	fresh, chopped, 1 teaspoon or 1/2 teaspoon dried
SQUABS	4, cleaned
BACON	4 slices, cut in half
STOCK	from giblets, 1/2 cup

Cook ONION in 1/3 cup BUTTER for 5 minutes. Mix with the next 5 ingredients. Stuff birds and skewer openings; place on a rack in a shallow pan. Cover breasts with BACON. Roast in a preheated 325°F. oven for 1 1/4 hours, basting with a mixture of STOCK and 1/4 cup melted BUTTER. After 1 hour remove BACON. Serves 4.

SOUR CREAM CRESS OMELET

| SOUR CREAM | 2 tablespoons |
| WATERCRESS | leaves, 1/4 cup, finely chopped |

EGGS	2
SALT	1/8 teaspoon
PEPPER	white, freshly ground, 1/16 teaspoon
WATER	2 teaspoons
BUTTER	1 tablespoon

Mix the SOUR CREAM and WATERCRESS together. Beat EGGS slightly with SALT, PEPPER and WATER. Heat omelet pan, add BUTTER and when it starts to sizzle immediately add EGGS. Agitate the pan back and forth and stir EGGS gently with the flat side of a fork. When EGGS begin to set, stir only the top surface. Remove from heat and let omelet set for a few seconds while loosening the edges. Spoon the SOUR CREAM-WATERCRESS mixture onto one half of the omelet and fold the other half over. Roll the omelet out onto a warm plate. Serves 1.

SCRAMBLED EGGS TARRAGON

CREAM	medium, 1/4 cup
BUTTER	2 tablespoons
CHEESE	Chevre or cream cheese, 1 1/2 ounces, at room temperature
EGGS	6
SALT	1/4 teaspoon
PEPPER	white, freshly ground, 1/4 teaspoon
TARRAGON	fresh, chopped, 1 teaspoon or 1/2 teaspoon dried

Heat the CREAM, BUTTER and CHEESE in a skillet. Break up the CHEESE with a fork and stir until smooth. Break the EGGS into the mixture and season with SALT and PEPPER. Cook until EGGS are soft scrambled. Serves 4.

BREADED CURRIED EGGS

| EGGS | 8, hard-cooked |
| SALT | |

birds of the courtyard

PEPPER
EGG   1, raw
OIL   1 tablespoon
VINEGAR   1 tablespoon
FLOUR
BREAD CRUMBS dry

Cut EGGS in half lengthwise and sprinkle with SALT and PEPPER. Beat raw EGG with OIL and VINEGAR. Dip EGG halves in FLOUR, coating thoroughly. Dip in EGG mixture, then BREAD CRUMBS; pat CRUMBS onto EGGS to coat thoroughly. In a skillet heat 1/4 inch of OIL and fry breaded EGGS until golden on each side; remove to a paper towel. Place EGGS, cut side down, on a round hot platter in a circle and pour over the CURRY SAUCE. Serves 4.

CURRY SAUCE

BUTTER   3 tablespoons
ONION   1 medium, finely chopped
CURRY POWDER   1 to 2 teaspoons
FLOUR   3 tablespoons
MILK   1 1/2 cups, hot
SALT
PEPPER

Melt BUTTER in a saucepan and cook ONION until tender but not brown. Stir in CURRY POWDER and cook 1 minute more. Stir in 3 tablespoons FLOUR and gradually add hot MILK, stirring constantly, until thickened. SALT and PEPPER to taste.

ANiMALS OF the hiLLs

The mountains skipped like rams, and the little hills like lambs.

PSALM 114:4

The Israelites were originally shepherds, and many of the old patriarchs including Isaac, Jacob and Moses spent years of their lives protecting goats and sheep on lonely hills. The Hebrews kept huge flocks in biblical times, since pasture land was free and unlimited and human wealth was measured by the size of one's herd. At the height of his power Job owned more than fourteen thousand sheep! In those days the word "cattle" meant not only cows and oxen, but also sheep, goats, camels, and even horses.

The fat-tailed sheep were especially prized, and every part of the animal was used by the thrifty people: wool for clothing, skin for leather and parchment, milk for food, meat for special feast days. Usually the young male ram was sacrificed since its loss would not affect the future prospects of the herd as would the loss of the female ewe. Sheep might be prepared in a cauldron for the usual meal, but the Passover lamb prepared on the last night in Egypt was specially prepared, for Moses ordered: "Eat not of it raw, nor sodden at all with water, but roast with fire" (Exodus 12:9).

Mutton was a favorite food of the well-to-do, for the poor could afford this luxury only on special feast days. According to the records of King Solomon's steward, the King's court consumed sheep at the astounding rate of one hundred a day!

ANiMALs OF the hiLLs

The goat was another valued animal. Traced as far back as 8500 BC, the goat may well be the first food animal ever domesticated by man. Its hair was woven into warm cloaks and tents, water bottles were made from its skin, and its rich milk nourished the hungry and thirsty:

The lambs are for thy clothing, and the goats are the price of the field.
And thou shalt have goats' milk enough for thy food, and for the food
of thy household.

Proverbs 27:26, 27

The succulent domesticated goat was highly prized for its taste and tenderness. Rebekah knew this well when she told her favored young son Jacob to win his father Isaac's blessing over his hunter brother Esau and bade him: "Go now to the flock, and fetch me from thence two good kids of the goats; and I will make them savory meat for thy father, such as he loveth" (Genesis 27:9).

When Jacob tricks Isaac into blessing him, Esau is off hunting venison. What kind of venison might the luckless Esau have captured to please the palate of his old blind father? Perhaps he sought the gazelle, the pyarg, or the chamois—all plentiful wild antelopes of the foothills. Or he might have hunted the roe deer, the hart, or the fallow deer of the forests of Galilee or Mount Carmel.

Wild hares were also fair game for the hunter's arrow. They were considered unclean by Mosaic law, for they were not cloven-footed, but the earliest Egyptians and Hebrews did enjoy their meat, and caught them in snares or nets as well. There may have been as many as five different kinds of hares in the land, though no one type is native to the Mediterranean area.

The wild boar headed the list of the abominations by the Hebrews and the Muslims and pigs were considered unclean animals. Making their homes in the dense thickets along the Jordan River and the Dead Sea, these wild swine roamed in herds, breeding and multiplying, living on roots, grapes, fruit, and mice in the farmer's fields. When man began to settle permanently, these animals were domesticated.

Many of the Mosaic food laws were based on sound concepts of health as well as on moral principles. With no refrigeration in the

149

warm climate, eating pork could easily have caused death or illness. To this day, the dietary habits of many Jewish people still honor these laws. Meat may not be eaten with milk, butter, or cheese and all animals must be thoroughly cooked.

No such dietary rules are found in the New Testament however, and as the Book of Mark says, "There is nothing from without a man, that entering into him, can defile him" (Mark 7:15). Many modern Hebrews touch hands with this idea, and eat meat and fish as varied as those enjoyed by their Christian brethren.

SKEWERED LAMB

LAMB	3 pounds, boned leg of lamb, trimmed of fat and gristle
ONION	1 large, sliced
OLIVE OIL	1 cup
VINEGAR	tarragon, 3 tablespoons
GARLIC	1 clove, crushed
BAY LEAF	1 large
OREGANO	1/2 teaspoon fresh chopped or 1/4 teaspoon dried
PEPPERCORNS	1 tablespoon
SALT	1 teaspoon
ONIONS	small, whole, white parboiled

Cut LAMB into 1 1/4 inch cubes and place in a bowl. Combine sliced ONIONS and the next 7 ingredients and pour over LAMB; cover and refrigerate several hours or overnight. On each of 6 skewers alternate meat and small whole ONIONS. Brush with marinade; broil 2 inches from heat 8 to 10 minutes, turning to brown on all sides. Baste with marinade several times during broiling. Serves 6.

LEBANON LAMB WITH APRICOTS

SALT	
PEPPER	
LAMB SHOULDER	4 pounds, boned, rolled
APRICOT PUREE	or apricot or peach jam, slightly thinned, 1/2 cup

APRICOT HALVES	12 fresh, or 6 peaches
PISTACHIO NUTS	shelled, chopped, 1/4 cup
DATES	12 pitted and stuffed with chopped pistachio nuts

SALT and PEPPER the LAMB and place in an open pan in a preheated 325 °F. oven; after 1 1/4 hours baste with APRICOT puree. Arrange the APRICOT HALVES hollow side up around the LAMB with the stuffed DATES in each hollow. Roast another 15 to 30 minutes depending on the desired doneness. Allow 25 minutes a pound. Serves 6.

ABEL'S LAMB

Rotisserie Lamb Riblets

LAMB BREAST	4 pounds
SALT	
PEPPER	
GARLIC	1 large clove, crushed
APRICOT JAM	1/2 cup
WATER	1/4 cup
HONEY	1 tablespoon

Sprinkle the LAMB BREAST with SALT and PEPPER and rub with GARLIC. Weave the meat onto rotisserie skewer. Keep meat 8 or more inches above slow coals. During the last half hour of cooking, brush often with apricot sauce made by mixing APRICOT JAM, WATER and HONEY together. When done, about 1 1/2 to 2 hours, remove from skewer and cut riblets into serving sized pieces. Serves 4 to 6.

ADAM'S STEW

Lamb And Bean Casserole

OIL	3 tablespoons
PORK	1/2 pound, cut into cubes
LAMB	1 pound, cut into cubes

ONIONS	2 medium, chopped
GARLIC	2 tablespoons, chopped
ROSEMARY	fresh, chopped, 1 teaspoon or 1/2 teaspoon dried
THYME LEAVES	fresh, chopped, 1 teaspoon or 1/2 teaspoon dried
SALT	1 teaspoon
PEPPER	freshly ground black, 1/8 teaspoon
WATER	1 cup
STOCK	lamb or beef, 1 cup
DRIED PEELED FAVA BEANS	or large lima beans, 2 cups, cooked until almost tender, reserving 1 1/2 cups bean liquid

Heat OIL and brown PORK cubes. Remove to a 3 quart casserole. Brown LAMB, ONIONS and GARLIC and add to PORK. Add herbs, seasoning and WATER to the casserole. Cover and bake in a preheated 350°F. oven for 1 hour. Add STOCK, BEANS and bean liquid. Cover and cook 30 minutes or until meat is tender. Correct seasoning. Serves 6.

LAMB CASSEROLE

LAMB	2 pounds, boned shank or shoulder, cut into 1 inch pieces
FLOUR	
OIL	4 tablespoons
ONION	1/2 cup, chopped
GARLIC	1 large clove, finely chopped
STOCK	lamb or beef, 2 1/2 cups, heated
SALT	1/2 teaspoon
PEPPER	freshly ground, 1/8 teaspoon
MARJORAM	fresh, chopped, 1/2 teaspoon or 1/4 teaspoon dried
FENNEL BULB	or celery, 1 cup, sliced
BULGUR	uncooked, 1 cup

Dredge the LAMB in FLOUR and brown in OIL. Transfer to a casserole and cook the ONION and GARLIC in remaining OIL. Add heated STOCK, SALT, PEPPER and MARJORAM. Pour into the casserole; cover and bake in a preheated 350°F. oven for 30 minutes. Stir in chopped FENNEL BULB and BULGUR. Cook 30 minutes longer or until meat is tender. Correct the seasoning. Serve with a conserve or chutney. Serves 6.

HAM AND EGG SALAD

WATERCRESS	1 bunch
LETTUCE	loose leaf, 1 head, torn into bite size pieces
HAM	2 cups cut into 1/4 inch cubes
EGGS	6, hard-cooked, whites chopped, yolks grated
GREEN ONIONS	6, thinly sliced
OLIVE OIL	3/4 cup
VINEGAR	tarragon, 6 tablespoons
MUSTARD	dry, 1 teaspoon
ANISE SEED	or caraway, 1/2 teaspoon

Arrange WATERCRESS and LETTUCE in a salad bowl. Mix the chopped HAM and EGG whites together and pile in the center; place ONION slices on top and sprinkle with grated EGG yolks. Mix the OIL, VINEGAR, MUSTARD and ANISE together. When ready to serve, pour the dressing over the salad and toss lightly. Serves 6.

ESAU'S ROTISSERIE VENISON

VENISON LEG	4 to 5 pounds, boned
GARLIC	2 large cloves, 1 crushed, 1 chopped
ONION	1 medium, chopped
JUNIPER BERRIES	1 tablespoon crushed
ERECH DRESSING	p. 182, or French dressing, 1 1/2 cups
GRAPE JUICE	1 1/2 cups
BACON	

Rub VENISON with crushed GARLIC. Combine chopped GARLIC, ONION and the remaining ingredients except BACON and pour over the meat. Let marinate several hours, basting with the marinade and turning the meat. Roll the meat as tightly as possible and tie at 1 1/2 inch intervals. Spear onto spit and wrap with slices of BACON secured with small metal skewers. Cook about 2 to 2 1/2 hours for medium rare. Baste often with the marinade. Serves 8 to 10.

VENISON STEW

VENISON	or beef, 3 pounds, boneless
FLOUR	
SALT	
PEPPER	
BACON FAT	3 tablespoons
ONIONS	2 large, chopped
GARLIC	2 large cloves, finely chopped
TARRAGON	fresh, chopped, 1/2 teaspoon or 1/4 teaspoon dried
STOCK	beef, 2 cups

Cut the meat into 1 1/4 inch cubes; dust with FLOUR, SALT and PEPPER. Brown the meat on all sides in BACON FAT over medium heat; add ONIONS and remaining ingredients. Cover and simmer about 1 1/2 hours or until very tender. Thicken gravy with FLOUR and water mixed into a paste, and correct the seasoning. Serves 6.

GADARA HARE

SALT	
PEPPER	
RABBIT	or chicken, 2 or 3 pounds, cut into serving pieces
FLOUR	

ANiMALs OF Che hiLLs

BUTTER	1/4 cup
ONIONS	2 large, sliced
GARLIC	3 large cloves, chopped
POMEGRANATE JUICE	or cranberry, 3/4 cup
STOCK	3/4 cup, from giblets
PARSLEY	2 tablespoons, chopped

SALT and PEPPER RABBIT and dust with FLOUR. Heat BUTTER in a skillet and brown RABBIT; remove from skillet and add ONIONS and GARLIC to skillet. Cook 5 minutes. Return RABBIT to skillet. Pour in POMEGRAN-ATE JUICE and STOCK; cover and simmer 1 hour or until tender. Turn the pieces several times during cooking and baste with the sauce. Remove RABBIT to a hot serving plate; skim off fat. Adjust the seasoning and pour the sauce over the RABBIT. Sprinkle with PARSLEY. Serves 4.

FRIED RABBIT

RABBIT	or chicken, 2 1/2 to 3 pounds, cut into serving pieces
GARLIC	1 large clove, crushed
MILK	1 cup
SALT	1 teaspoon
PEPPER	1/4 teaspoon
FLOUR	1 cup
GINGER	ground, 1 1/2 teaspoons
BUTTER	1/4 cup
OIL	1/4 cup
STOCK	chicken, 1/2 cup
SOUR CREAM	1/2 cup
CHIVES	1 tablespoon, finely chopped
PARSLEY	1 tablespoon, finely chopped

Rub the RABBIT pieces with GARLIC and put in a bowl. Pour the MILK over and let stand for 30 minutes; drain and reserve MILK. SALT and PEPPER RABBIT and dip in combined FLOUR and GINGER. In a large skillet brown the pieces of RABBIT on all sides in the BUTTER-OIL mixture. Reduce heat and cook, covered, about 45 minutes or until tender; remove to a warm platter. Drain off all but 3 tablespoons fat and add 3 tablespoons FLOUR to the pan drippings; cook 1 minute and stir in MILK and STOCK. When thickened add SOUR CREAM; stir in CHIVES and PARSLEY and heat, but do not boil. Pour the sauce over the RABBIT. Serves 4.

HAZOR ROAST
Stuffed Pork

PORK LOIN ROAST	about 6 pounds
SALT	
GARLIC	1 large clove, crushed
SHILOH STUFFING	p. 181
BUTTER	1 tablespoon
APRICOT JUICE	1/2 cup
HONEY	1/4 cup

Form a deep pocket by cutting along ribs of the PORK LOIN starting 1 inch away from end of roast and ending 1 inch away from the other end; cut almost to the bottom of the roast. Rub SALT and GARLIC on outside of roast and inside the pocket. Stuff pocket with SHILOH STUFFING and dot the top with BUTTER; cover opening with a piece of foil to keep from drying out. Left over stuffing may be baked in a separate pan, covered, for 30 minutes. Bake roast in a preheated 350°F. oven for about 3 1/2 hours or until 170°F. on a meat thermometer. Mix APRICOT JUICE and HONEY together and baste several times during the last half hour of baking. Serves 8.

RIBS OF JOPPA
Grilled Spareribs

ERECH DRESSING   p. 182, or French dressing, 3/4 cup

ANiMALs of the hiLLs

PARSLEY	1 tablespoon, finely chopped
ROSEMARY	fresh, chopped, 1/2 teaspoon or 1/4 teaspoon dried
SAVORY	fresh, chopped, 1 teaspoon or 1/2 teaspoon dried
MUSTARD	dry, 1/2 teaspoon
HONEY	3 tablespoons
PORK SPARERIBS	4 pounds

Combine all the ingredients except the SPARERIBS and mix well. Pour the marinade over the RIBS and refrigerate several hours or overnight. Drain; reserve marinade. Place RIBS on grill 8 inches above source of heat. Baste and turn until crisp, about 1 1/2 to 2 hours, or until no pink shows when cut between bones. Slow cooking makes the RIBS more juicy.

ALEXANDRIA MEAT LOAF

Ham Roquefort Loaf

ONION	1 large, finely chopped
BUTTER	2 tablespoons
EGGS	2, slightly beaten
MILK	3/4 cup
PEPPER	freshly ground white, 1/8 teaspoon
CLOVES	ground, 1/8 teaspoon
BREAD CRUMBS	fine, 1 cup
ROQUEFORT CHEESE	3/4 cup, crumbled
PORK	lean, ground, 1 pound
HAM	lean, ground, 1 pound

In a small frying pan cook ONION in BUTTER for 5 minutes; reserve. Combine EGGS and the next 4 ingredients in a bowl; let stand 10 minutes. Add 1/2 cup ROQUEFORT CHEESE, meats and ONION; mix well. Press into a 9 × 5 × 3 inch pan. Bake in a preheated 350°F. oven for 1 1/2 hours. Drain; remove from pan and place on a rack. Top with remaining CHEESE. Broil 4 inches from heat until lightly browned. Serves 6.

HAM AND SPINACH CASSEROLE

ONION	1 large, finely chopped
HAM FAT	rendered, 2 tablespoons or oil
FLOUR	2 tablespoons
SPINACH	3 cups, cooked, chopped; reserve 1/3 cup cooking liquid
CREAM	light, 1/2 cup
MACE	ground, 1/4 teaspoon
SALT	
PEPPER	
HAM	ground, 2 cups, cooked
ROMANO CHEESE	or Parmesan, 1/4 cup, grated

Cook the ONION in the HAM FAT for 5 minutes; blend in the FLOUR and 1/3 cup of SPINACH liquid. Cook, over low heat, until smooth and thickened; stir in the CREAM, MACE and SPINACH. SALT and PEPPER to taste. Spoon the SPINACH into a 1 1/2 quart shallow casserole and fold in the HAM. Sprinkle with ROMANO CHEESE and bake in a preheated 400°F. oven for 15 to 20 minutes or until well heated. Serves 4 to 6.

FRIED PIGS' FEET

PIGS' FEET	4, fresh, split in half lengthwise
FLOUR	
EGG	1, beaten
VINEGAR	tarragon, 1 tablespoon
SALT	1/4 teaspoon
PEPPER	freshly ground
MUSTARD	dry, 1/4 teaspoon
MARJORAM	fresh, chopped, 1/2 teaspoon or 1/4 teaspoon dried
BREAD CRUMBS	fine, dry
OIL	
PARSLEY	

Wash PIGS' FEET. Cover with salted water and simmer 2 hours or until tender; cool and drain. Dredge in FLOUR, dip in EGG mixed with the next 5 ingredients and then in BREAD CRUMBS. Add OIL to a skillet and fry the PIGS'

FEET on both sides until golden. Serve with CHIVE SAUCE (p. 159). Serves 4.

CHIVE SAUCE

JAVAN DRESSING	p. 183, or mayonnaise, 1 cup
VINEGAR	tarragon, 2 tablespoons
MUSTARD	dry, 1 teaspoon
ONION JUICE	1 teaspoon
RADISH	1 tablespoon, grated
CHIVES	1 tablespoon, finely chopped

Blend the first 2 ingredients together. Mix the remaining ingredients and combine. Makes about 1 cup.

STUFFED LAMB BREAST

OIL	1 tablespoon
GREEN ONIONS	1/2 cup, chopped
BREAD CRUMBS	day old, 2 cups, about 8 thin slices
ANCHOVIES	flat, 2 ounces, drained and chopped
PARSLEY	1/2 cup, chopped
ROSEMARY LEAVES	fresh, chopped, 1/2 teaspoon or 1/4 teaspoon dried
EGG	1, beaten
PEPPER	freshly ground, 1/4 teaspoon
GARLIC	1 large clove, crushed
LAMB BREAST	2 one pound pieces
RADISHES	
PARSLEY	

Cook GREEN ONIONS in OIL for 5 minutes and add to the BREAD CRUMBS with the next 3 ingredients; mix well. Add the EGG and PEPPER and toss lightly. Rub the meat on both sides with the GARLIC; thinly slice the GARLIC and place slivers in scored surface of the LAMB BREAST. Place stuffing between the two pieces of meat and tie or skewer together. Roast in a preheated 350°F. oven for about 1 3/4 hours or until done. Remove string or skewers and serve on a heated platter. Garnish with RADISHES and PARSLEY. Serves 4.

KING SOLOMON'S POACHED LAMB WITH CAPER SAUCE

LEG OF LAMB	or mutton, about 6 pounds
WATER	
ONION	1 medium, stuck with 3 cloves
BAY LEAF	1 large
PEPPERCORNS	2 teaspoons
FENNEL BULB	2 slices 1/4 inch thick or 1 rib of celery
SALT	
WATERCRESS	
CAPER SAUCE	

Remove fat from leg of LAMB and trim skin. Place in a kettle and cover with WATER; simmer 10 minutes over low heat, skimming several times. Add the next 4 ingredients and simmer for 1 hour. Add SALT to taste and continue to simmer until tender. Drain, reserving the broth for a future soup base. Remove LAMB to a heated platter and garnish with WATERCRESS. Serve with barley, groats or bulgur and CAPER SAUCE. Cook lamb 15 to 20 minutes per pound. Serves 10 to 12.

CAPER SAUCE

BUTTER	1/4 cup
FLOUR	1/4 cup
SALT	1/2 teaspoon
PEPPER	freshly ground white, 1/4 teaspoon
MILK	1 cup
STOCK	lamb or mutton, 1 cup
CAPERS	2 tablespoons

Melt BUTTER, stir in FLOUR, SALT and PEPPER; cook 1 minute. Add MILK and STOCK and cook, stirring constantly, until sauce is smooth and thickened. Stir in CAPERS. Makes 2 cups.

ANiMALS OF
the pASCURELANd

And Abraham ran unto the herd, and fecht
a calf tender and good.

GENESIS 18:7

Beef was seldom eaten, because cows and oxen were too valuable for ploughing fields to be used for meat. Only the rich owned them in any great numbers. The wealthy cattle owners could afford to select choice young animals from the herd and feed them special fodder for the table, keeping them in stalls to fatten. This was a great luxury however, one which the prophet Amos warns against, upbraiding the rich men who

> *lie upon beds of ivory, and stretch themselves upon their couches, and*
> *eat lambs out of the flock and the calves out of the midst of the stall.*
> *Amos 6:4.*

Yet there were special occasions, such as the arrival of a long awaited guest, when the calf was taken from the field and feasted upon. After God promised the hundred-year-old Abraham that his wife Sarah would yet bear him a son, the old patriarch royally entertained three men sent of the Lord:

> *And Abraham ran unto the herd, and fetcht a calf tender and good,*
> *and gave it unto a young man: and he hasted to dress it. And he took*
> *butter, and milk, and the calf which he had dressed, and set it before*

biblical garden cookery

them; and he stood by them under the tree and they did eat.

Genesis 18:7–8.

And later, in the New Testament, Christ tells the parable of the prodigal son and describes the great rejoicing and feasting when the young man returns, poor and broken, to his home. So thankful is the father for the safety of his beloved child that he orders his servants to "bring hither the fatted calf and kill it and let us eat and be merry" (Luke 15:23).

PHILIPPI STUFFED FLANK STEAK

ONION	1 cup, chopped
GARLIC	1 large clove, chopped
SALT	3/4 teaspoon
PEPPER	freshly ground, 1/8 teaspoon
SAVORY	fresh, chopped, 1 teaspoon or 1/2 teaspoon dried
THYME	fresh, chopped, 1 teaspoon or 1/2 teaspoon dried
CORIANDER LEAVES	or parsley, 1 tablespoon, chopped
OIL	
BREAD CRUMBS	fine, dry, 1 1/2 cups
FLANK STEAK	2 to 3 pounds

Cook the first 7 ingredients in 2 tablespoons OIL in large skillet for 3 to 4 minutes; add BREAD CRUMBS and mix lightly. Pound FLANK STEAK with a mallet and spread the stuffing on the meat. Roll meat lengthwise and tie in several places with a string. Add 2 tablespoons OIL to the pan and brown meat. Place on a rack in a baking pan and roast in a preheated 300°F. oven for 2 hours or until tender. Remove string and serve on a hot platter. Carve diagonally across the grain of the meat. Serves 6.

BRAISED STEAK SAMUEL

CHUCK STEAK	or round, 2 to 2 1/2 pounds
FLOUR	1/3 cup
SALT	1 teaspoon

ANiMALS OF The PASTURELAND

PEPPER	1/4 teaspoon, freshly ground
OIL	3 tablespoons
STOCK	beef, 2 1/2 cups
GARLIC	1 large clove, finely chopped
CURRY POWDER	2 teaspoons
ONION	1/4 cup, chopped
GOLDEN APPLE CONSERVE	or chutney, 1/2 cup
RAISINS	golden, 1/4 cup

Cut meat into serving size pieces. Mix FLOUR, SALT and PEPPER together; rub into all sides of the meat. Heat OIL in a skillet and brown meat. Add beef STOCK and the remaining ingredients; cover. Simmer 2 to 2 1/2 hours or until meat is tender. Serve with bulgur or groats. Serves 6.

MEAT LOAF MASADA

BEEF	1 pound, lean, ground
BREAD CRUMBS	1 cup, soft
ROMANO CHEESE	1/2 cup, grated
ONION	2 tablespoons, finely chopped
PARSLEY	1/4 cup, chopped
GARLIC	1/4 teaspoon, finely chopped
SALT	1 3/4 teaspoons
OREGANO	1 1/4 teaspoons, dried
PEPPER	1/2 teaspoon, freshly ground
EGGS	3 large
OIL	2 teaspoons
BREAD CRUMBS	2 to 3 tablespoons, fine, dry
COTTAGE CHEESE	1/2 pound

Combine the first 6 ingredients. Add 1 1/2 teaspoons of the SALT, 1 teaspoon of the OREGANO, 1/4 teaspoon of the PEPPER and 2 beaten EGGS; mix well. Grease a 8 1/2 × 4 1/2 × 2 5/8 inch pan with OIL and sprinkle with fine dry BREAD CRUMBS. Turn 1/2 of the meat mixture into the pan and spread evenly. Mix remaining 1/4 teaspoon SALT, OREGANO, PEPPER and beaten EGG with the COT-

TAGE CHEESE. Spread over meat. Top with remaining meat mixture, covering cheese completely. Bake in a preheated 350°F. oven for about 1 1/4 hours or until the loaf pulls away from the sides of the pan. Let cool 10 minutes in the pan; drain off any liquid and turn out onto a warm platter. Serves 8.

BRAISED BEEF

BEEF	chuck or top round, boneless, 2 pounds, cut into 1 1/2 inch cubes
FLOUR	1/3 cup
OIL	2 tablespoons
SALT	2 teaspoons
PEPPER	1/4 teaspoon, freshly ground
GARLIC	2 large cloves, chopped
STOCK	beef, 2 1/4 cups
BAY LEAF	1 large
MARJORAM	fresh, chopped, 1/2 teaspoon or 1/4 teaspoon dried
THYME	fresh, chopped, 1 teaspoon or 1/2 teaspoon dried
PARSLEY	2 tablespoons, chopped

Dredge the BEEF with FLOUR and brown on all sides in OIL in a casserole. Add SALT and PEPPER and the remaining ingredients, except PARSLEY. Cover and simmer 2 to 2 1/2 hours or until meat is tender; stir occasionally. Sprinkle with PARSLEY before serving. Serves 4 to 6.

BRAISED SHORT RIBS OF BEEF GOSHEN

SALT	
PEPPER	
BEEF SHORT RIBS	3 pounds, cut into 3 inch pieces
FLOUR	
OIL	2 tablespoons
STOCK	beef, 2 cups
ONIONS	small, whole, 8

CREAM	heavy, 1/2 cup
SOUR CREAM	1/4 cup
RADISHES	2 tablespoons, finely chopped
MUSTARD	dry, 1 teaspoon
PARSLEY	2 tablespoons, chopped

SALT and PEPPER the SHORT RIBS and dredge with FLOUR. In a casserole brown the meat in OIL on all sides; add STOCK. Cover and cook in a preheated 300°F. oven for 2 hours or until very tender. Baste frequently with liquid in casserole. Add the ONIONS during the last half hour. Remove meat and ONIONS to a hot platter. Stir in the CREAM, SOUR CREAM, RADISHES and MUSTARD and cook over low heat just long enough to warm CREAM; do not boil. Pour over RIBS and sprinkle with PARSLEY. Serves 4.

HONEY GLAZED CORNED BEEF

CORNED BEEF	5 pounds of brisket
WATER	to cover
PICKLING SPICES	1 tablespoon
WHOLE CLOVES	
MUSTARD	1 tablespoon, dry
WATER	2 tablespoons
VINEGAR	tarragon, 2 teaspoons
HONEY	1/4 cup
ALLSPICE	1/4 teaspoon, ground

Place meat in a large kettle with enough WATER to cover; add PICKLING SPICES. Bring to a boil; reduce heat and simmer, covered, about 4 hours or until meat is tender. Remove meat; drain and place on a rack in a shallow baking pan, fat side up. Score fat and stud with WHOLE CLOVES. Mix MUSTARD with WATER, VINEGAR and ALLSPICE; stir into HONEY. Spoon half the glaze over the meat. Bake in a preheated 350°F. oven 20 minutes. Remove from oven and spoon over remaining glaze; bake 20 minutes more or until meat is brown. Serves 8.

VEAL MARIAMNE
Roast Veal with Oyster Stuffing

OYSTERS	medium, 1/2 pint, and their liquor
BREAD CRUMBS	soft, 2 cups, lightly toasted
GREEN ONIONS	2 tablespoons, chopped
MACE	or nutmeg, 1/8 teaspoon
SALT	
PEPPER	
VEAL SHOULDER	4 to 5 pounds with pocket for stuffing
GARLIC	1 large clove, crushed
STOCK	chicken, 3/4 cup
BUTTER	melted, 3 tablespoons
GROATS HEROD	

Remove any bits of shell from OYSTERS and reserve liquor; coarsely chop OYSTERS. Toss OYSTERS, BREAD CRUMBS, GREEN ONIONS and MACE together; add SALT and PEPPER to taste. Moisten mixture with OYSTER liquor; spoon stuffing into VEAL pocket and sew or close with skewers. Rub VEAL with GARLIC. Place in shallow pan and pour over STOCK mixed with BUTTER. Roast in preheated 325° oven until meat thermometer registers 170° or 40 minutes per pound. Baste frequently with pan juices. Serve with GROATS HEROD. Serves 6.

GROATS HEROD

BUCKWHEAT GROATS	or kasha, 1 cup
BEEF STOCK	or water, 2 1/2 cups, boiling
SALT	1 teaspoon
BUTTER	1/4 cup
PEPPER	freshly ground

Heat large ungreased skillet and add BUCKWHEAT GROATS. Cook over medium heat until toasted, about 3 to 5 minutes, stirring and shaking pan constantly. Add STOCK, SALT and 2 tablespoons BUTTER. Cover tightly. Reduce heat and simmer 10 minutes; stir with fork. Cook 10 minutes more until grain is tender and STOCK is absorbed. Add remaining BUTTER and PEPPER to taste. Serves 4 to 6.

COLD ROLLED STUFFED BREAST OF VEAL

BREAST OF VEAL	boned, 3 1/2 pounds, before bones are removed, reserve bones
SALT	
PEPPER	
GARLIC	1 large clove, crushed
EGGS	8, hard-cooked
HAM	1/2 cup, finely chopped
RAISINS	3 tablespoons
PARSLEY	2 tablespoons, chopped
PISTACHIO NUTS	3 tablespoons, chopped
TARRAGON	fresh, chopped, 1 teaspoon or 1/2 teaspoon dried
MARJORAM	fresh, chopped, 1 teaspoon or 1/2 teaspoon dried
ONION	1 large, stuck with 1 clove
FENNEL BULB	2 thick slices or 1 rib celery
BAY LEAF	1 large
WATER	2 cups
WATERCRESS	

Lay VEAL skin side down and rub with SALT, PEPPER and GARLIC. Grate the EGGS into a bowl and add the next 6 ingredients; mix well with SALT and PEPPER to taste. Spread the mixture on the VEAL; roll and tie with string. Wrap in double thickness of cheesecloth, hold in place with string and tie ends securely. Place bones in bottom of a kettle with the veal roll on top. Add the last 4 ingredients and 1 teaspoon SALT. Cover and simmer over low heat for 2 hours. Cool meat in stock; remove meat, discard bones and vegetables and save stock for future use. Remove cheesecloth and refrigerate veal overnight. When ready to serve, slice the meat and arrange on a round platter overlapping the slices. Garnish with WATERCRESS in the center. Serves 6.

BROILED SKEWERED SPICED BEEF

BEEF	1 1/2 pounds ground chuck
ONION	3 tablespoons, finely chopped
OIL	1 1/2 tablespoons
SALT	1 1/2 teaspoons
CUMIN	3/4 teaspoon
CORIANDER	3/4 teaspoon
CINNAMON	1/4 teaspoon
PARSLEY	2 tablespoons, finely chopped

Combine all ingredients except PARSLEY; shape into 1 1/2 inch balls and thread onto skewers. Broil over charcoal or under broiler, turning to brown on all sides. Sprinkle PARSLEY over. Serves 6.

VEAL AND PORK BAKE

VEAL	1 pound from leg, cut into 1 1/4 inch cubes
PORK	1 pound, tenderloin, cut into 1 1/4 inch cubes
SALT	
PEPPER	
MUSTARD	dry, 1 teaspoon
THYME	fresh, chopped, 1/4 teaspoon or 1/8 teaspoon dried
MARJORAM	fresh, chopped, 1/4 teaspoon or 1/8 teaspoon dried
FLOUR	1/2 cup
OIL	1/4 cup
ONIONS	4 medium, quartered
WATER	hot, 2 cups
PARSLEY	

Season the meat with SALT and PEPPER. Mix the MUSTARD, THYME, MARJORAM and FLOUR together; dredge the meat with the seasoned FLOUR. Brown the meat in the OIL on all sides; cool and thread on short wooden skewers alternating the PORK and VEAL. Arrange the skewers on a baking pan and add ONIONS and WATER; cover and bake in a preheated 350°F. oven for 1 1/4 hours or until done. Arrange the skewers over a mound of groats or bulgur. Garnish with PARSLEY. Serves 4 to 6.

FRESH MINTED GRILLED PATTIES

VEAL	1 pound, ground
LAMB	1/2 pound, ground
MINT	fresh, chopped, 3 1/2 teaspoons or 3/4 teaspoon, dried
OREGANO	fresh, chopped, 1 teaspoon or 1/2 teaspoon dried
SALT	1 1/2 teaspoons
PEPPER	1/4 teaspoon
ONION JUICE	1 tablespoon

Combine all ingredients and mix well. Form into 8 patties and grill until done. Serve with yogurt. Serves 4.

VEAL RING

VEAL	2 1/2 pounds, ground
SALT PORK	1/2 pound, ground
BREAD CRUMBS	fine, 1 1/4 cups or crushed unsalted crackers
EGGS	2, slightly beaten
STOCK	chicken, 1/3 cup
SAGE	2 teaspoons
SALT	1 1/2 teaspoons
PEPPER	freshly ground, 1/4 teaspoon

Mix the first 3 ingredients together; combine EGGS with the remaining ingredients and work into the meat mixture. Pack into a 6 cup ring mold. Cover top with foil and bake in a preheated 350°F. oven for 1 hour; bake another 30 minutes uncovered. Remove from oven and let cool in the pan for 10 minutes; drain off liquid and turn onto a serving dish. Fill center with any hot vegetables. Serves 8 to 10.

VEAL LOAF

VEAL	2 pounds, ground
SALT PORK	1/4 pound, ground
BREAD CRUMBS	dry, 1/2 cup
SALT	2 teaspoons
PEPPER	1/4 teaspoon, freshly ground
CREAM	medium, 1/4 cup
TARRAGON LEAVES	fresh, chopped, 1/2 teaspoon or 1/4 teaspoon dried
EGGS	2
WATER	1/4 cup

Combine all ingredients except WATER. Mix thoroughly and place in a 8 1/2 × 4 1/2 × 2 5/8 inch loaf pan. Pour the WATER over the top. Bake in a preheated 350°F. oven for 1 to 1 1/4 hours. The loaf is done when it shrinks from sides of the pan. Serve with SAUCE MELITA (p.181). Serves 6.

FRICASSEE OF VEAL MEDEBA

WATER	2 quarts
VEAL KNUCKLES	2, cracked
VEAL	2 pounds, boneless, stewing, cut into 1 1/2 inch cubes
ONIONS	2 medium, quartered
FENNEL BULB	3 slices or 1 rib celery, chopped
SALT	1 tablespoon
PEPPER	freshly ground white, 1/8 teaspoon
FLOUR	2 tablespoons
VINEGAR	tarragon, 3 tablespoons
HONEY	or sugar, 1 teaspoon
NUTMEG	1/8 teaspoon
EGG	1, slightly beaten
PARSLEY	2 tablespoons, chopped

Bring the WATER to boil in a kettle and add the KNUCK-LES, VEAL and the next 4 ingredients; simmer slowly for 2 hours. Strain and reserve the stock. Remove the VEAL, discarding the bones, ONIONS and FENNEL slices. Place meat in a saucepan with 2 cups of the reserved stock; save remaining stock for future soup. Mix a paste of FLOUR and VINEGAR and add to meat stock; cook until thickened, stirring constantly. Add HONEY and NUTMEG. Just before serving, stir in the EGG and cook for 1 minute over low heat. Garnish with chopped PARSLEY. Serves 6.

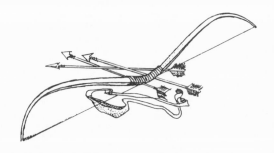

hUNTER'S REWARD

Thou huntest me as a fierce lion.
JOB 10:16

In biblical times, hunting animals was not a sport but a necessity. Wild animals were killed, not only for food, but to protect the flocks and other domesticated livestock. Man, with his superior intelligence, used nets, pits, knives, spears, and arrows for the killing of these intruders. Egyptian kings were the exceptions, for they hunted with bow and arrow for sport.

A custom, from the beginning of time, is the "reward of the hunter" who brings down the wild animal and is then entitled to the liver. It is eaten warm, cut out of the newly killed beast, but only after the blood has been poured out after the laws of Deuteronomy 12:16 and Leviticus 17:13.

Today we tend to overlook the liver and other organs as being too time consuming and difficult to prepare. But they are delicious and full of nutrition, a rewarding contribution to any meal.

HEARTS HAURAN
Stuffed Veal Hearts

APRICOT DATE STUFFING

BUTTER	6 tablespoons
ONION	1/2 cup, finely chopped
APRICOT	dried, 1/4 cup, finely chopped
DATES	pitted, 1/4 cup, finely chopped
BREAD CRUMBS	day old, 2 cups
SALT	1/4 teaspoon
PEPPER	freshly ground, white
MINT	3 tablespoons fresh, chopped or 1 1/2 tablespoons dried
WATER	2 to 3 tablespoons

Cook ONIONS in 2 tablespoons BUTTER for 5 minutes. Add APRICOTS and DATES; cook 3 minutes. Add remaining BUTTER, BREAD CRUMBS, SALT, PEPPER, MINT and WATER; toss lightly and remove from heat. Reserve.

HEARTS

VEAL HEARTS	4, about 3/4 pound each
SALT	
PEPPER	freshly ground white
GARLIC	1 large clove
BUTTER	2 tablespoons
WATER	1 1/4 cups
FLOUR	2 teaspoons
CREAM	medium, 1 cup
PARSLEY	

Trim HEARTS and remove fat and tubes. Sprinkle with SALT and PEPPER and rub with GARLIC, inside and out. Stuff HEARTS dividing the stuffing equally between them; sew opening together. In a heavy casserole, brown HEARTS in BUTTER on all sides. Add WATER, bring to a boil and place in a preheated 325°F. oven for 1 1/2 hours or until tender. Check after 1 hour and add a little WATER if necessary. Remove HEARTS to a serving platter, pull out the threads and slice 1/2 inch thick. Stir FLOUR into remaining juices; add CREAM and cook over low heat until thickened. Correct seasoning. Pour over HEARTS. Garnish with PARSLEY. Serves 6.

TONGUES CORINTH
Tongues In Spiced Sauce

CALVES' TONGUES	4, about 7 to 8 ounces each
WATER	
GARLIC	3 cloves, large, chopped
ONION	1 medium, stuck with 2 whole cloves
SALT	1 teaspoon
PEPPERCORNS	black, 1/4 teaspoon
FENNEL SEEDS	
CORIANDER SEED	1/4 teaspoon, ground
CUMIN SEED	
BUTTER	1/4 cup
SHALLOTS	or green onions, 4, finely chopped
FLOUR	3 tablespoons
STOCK	beef, 2 cups
BASIL	fresh, chopped, 1/2 teaspoon or 1/4 teaspoon dried
TARRAGON	fresh, chopped, 1/2 teaspoon or 1/4 teaspoon dried
MACE	or nutmeg, 1/8 teaspoon, ground

Put TONGUES in a kettle with WATER to cover. Add GARLIC, ONION, SALT, PEPPERCORNS and the next 3 spices. Bring to a boil, cover and simmer 1 hour. Remove TONGUES and peel off skins and roots. Melt BUTTER in a casserole and brown the TONGUES; remove to a plate. Add SHALLOTS to casserole and cook 5 minutes. Stir in FLOUR, add STOCK and cook until thickened. Return the TONGUES to the casserole and add BASIL, TARRAGON and MACE. Cover and place in a preheated 350°F. oven and bake for 1 hour or until the TONGUES are very tender. Serve in the casserole. Serves 4.

TIMOTHY'S CHOICE
Veal Kidneys

VEAL KIDNEYS	4
GARLIC	1 large clove, finely chopped
BUTTER	3 tablespoons
SALT	
PEPPER	freshly ground
STOCK	chicken, 6 tablespoons
PARSLEY	3 tablespoons, finely chopped
ANCHOVIES	8, finely chopped
TOAST	4 slices, cut into triangles

Cut away any fat and peel membrane from KIDNEYS; slice 1/2 inch thick. Remove the center core with scissors. Cook KIDNEYS and GARLIC in BUTTER, over medium heat, for 5 minutes, stirring often. Season with SALT and PEPPER. Stir in STOCK, PARSLEY and ANCHOVIES. Cook 1 or 2 minutes more; KIDNEYS become tough if overcooked. Arrange KIDNEYS on buttered TOAST and pour over pan juice. Serves 4.

BAKED SWEETBREADS

SWEETBREADS	3 pair, precooked
BUTTER	1/4 cup, melted
GARLIC	1 medium clove, finely chopped
ONION	1/2 cup, chopped
RADISHES	1/2 cup, chopped
BAY LEAF	1 medium
TARRAGON	fresh, chopped, 1 teaspoon or 1/2 teaspoon dried
PARSLEY	1/4 cup, chopped
STOCK	beef, 1 cup
SALT	1 teaspoon

Prepare SWEETBREADS as soon as purchased by placing them in cold water and soaking for 1/2 hour. Drain and simmer in salted water to cover, with 1 tablespoon vinegar, for 15 minutes. Drain and plunge SWEETBREADS into cold water to keep them white and firm. Cut and discard tissue that connects them. Pat dry. Put BUTTER in a casserole, add the next 6 ingredients and cook, over low heat, until ONIONS are soft. Lay the SWEETBREADS on top of the vegetables; add STOCK and SALT. Place in a preheated 350°F. oven and bake for 30 minutes, basting occasionally with the pan juices. Serves 6.

BRAINS NICOPOLIS

Calf's Brains with Curried Javan Dressing

CURRIED JAVAN DRESSING

GARLIC	1/4 teaspoon, minced
SALT	1/4 teaspoon
PEPPER	freshly ground white
CORIANDER SEED	1/4 teaspoon, ground
CUMIN SEED	1/4 teaspoon, ground
MUSTARD	dry, 1/4 teaspoon
OLIVE OIL	1 tablespoon
JAVAN DRESSING	p. 183, 1/2 cup
PARSLEY	1 tablespoon, finely chopped

To make curry, pound GARLIC with SALT, PEPPER and spices in a mortar or crush with wooden spoon in a bowl; mix in OIL. In a small pan or aluminum measuring cup, cook the curry for 1 minute over low heat, stirring continually. Cool; stir into JAVAN DRESSING. Fold in the PARSLEY; reserve.

BRAINS

BRAINS	4 veal brains, about 1/4 pound each
SALT	2 teaspoons
WATER	
VINEGAR	tarragon, 2 teaspoons
JAVAN DRESSING	curried, 1/2 cup
EGG	1 hard-cooked, yolk and white grated separately
WATERCRESS	
OLIVES	black, preferably Greek

Soak BRAINS in cold water with 1 teaspoon SALT and 1 teaspoon VINEGAR for 15 minutes; drain. Peel off the membrane carefully with fingers. Put in a saucepan of boiling WATER to cover and add remaining SALT and VINEGAR; simmer 12 to 15 minutes. Drain, plunge into cold WATER, drain and pat dry with a paper towel. Cover with plastic wrap and refrigerate until cold. When ready to serve, place BRAINS on a serving dish. Coat each with CURRIED JAVAN DRESSING. Sprinkle with the grated EGG white and top with EGG yolk. Garnish with WATERCRESS and OLIVES. Serves 4 as an appetizer or salad.

BAKED CALF'S LIVER

ONION	1 medium, finely chopped
BUTTER	1/4 cup
BREAD CRUMBS	fresh, 2 cups
SALT	1/2 teaspoon
PEPPER	freshly ground, 1/4 teaspoon
THYME	fresh, chopped, 1/4 teaspoon or 1/8 teaspoon dried
MARJORAM	fresh, chopped, 1/4 teaspoon or 1/8 teaspoon dried
EGG	1, lightly beaten
CALF'S LIVER	or beef, 6 thick slices
BACON	6 slices

Cook ONION in BUTTER until lightly browned. Add to BREAD CRUMBS, seasonings and EGG and mix well. Cut a pocket in each slice of LIVER and fill with stuffing. Place LIVER slices in a buttered baking dish and put a slice of BACON on top of each. Bake in a preheated 350°F. oven for 30 to 40 minutes, depending on the desired doneness. Baste often with pan juices. Serves 6.

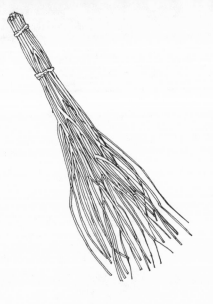

ODDMENTS

. . . for a sweetsmelling savour.
EPHESIANS 5:2

As all biblical cooks from Rebekah to Martha knew, meals are made most savory by the addition of stuffings, dressings and sauces.

BREAD AND SHALLOT STUFFING

BUTTER	5 tablespoons
SHALLOTS	1 cup, finely chopped
PARSLEY	1/4 cup, chopped
TARRAGON	fresh, chopped, 1 teaspoon or 1/2 teaspoon dried
BREAD CRUMBS	soft, 4 cups
WATER	
SALT	
PEPPER	

Melt BUTTER and cook the SHALLOTS, PARSLEY and TARRAGON over medium heat for 5 minutes. Add

BREAD CRUMBS and toss lightly; add WATER to moisten. SALT and PEPPER to taste. Use for game, poultry or fish.

SHILOH STUFFING
Watercress Stuffing

ONIONS	1/2 cup, chopped
BUTTER	1/4 cup
WATERCRESS	1 1/2 cups, chopped
SALT	1/2 teaspoon
PEPPER	freshly ground white, 1/8 teaspoon
BREAD CUBES	4 cups, firm white or whole wheat, 2 days old, cut into 1/4 inch cubes
PISTACHIO NUTS	or almonds, 1/4 cup, chopped
STOCK	chicken

Cook ONIONS in BUTTER over medium heat for 5 minutes. Add WATERCRESS, SALT and PEPPER. Combine in a bowl the BREAD CUBES and PISTACHIO NUTS; add the ONION and WATERCRESS mixture and toss lightly. Moisten with STOCK and toss until thoroughly mixed. Recipe will stuff a 4 pound chicken, or use half the recipe for a 3 to 4 pound fish.

KEDAR MARINADE
Mint Marinade

MINT	2 tablespoons chopped fresh or 1 tablespoon dried, crumbled
OLIVE OIL	1/2 cup
APRICOT JUICE	3/4 cup
VINEGAR	tarragon, 6 tablespoons
HONEY	2 tablespoons
SALT	1 teaspoon
GARLIC	2 cloves, crushed

Combine all ingredients in a saucepan and bring to a boil; simmer 2 minutes. Remove from heat. Let steep 30 minutes; cool and strain before using. Makes enough to marinate 3 pounds of cubed meat, about 1 3/4 cups.

SARAH'S SAUCE

ONION JUICE	2 teaspoons
SALT	2 teaspoons
MUSTARD	dry, 1 teaspoon
SOUR CREAM	1 1/2 cups
CUCUMBER	1/2 cup, peeled, seeded, minced
RADISH	1/4 cup, minced
SALT	
PEPPER	

Mix the first 3 ingredients into a paste and stir into the SOUR CREAM. Fold in the drained CUCUMBER and RADISHES. SALT and PEPPER to taste. Makes about 2 1/2 cups.

TARRAGON SAUCE

BUTTER	3 tablespoons
FLOUR	3 tablespoons
SALT	1/2 teaspoon
PEPPER	1/8 teaspoon, freshly ground
TARRAGON LEAVES	fresh, chopped, 2 teaspoons or 1 teaspoon dried
PARSLEY	2 teaspoons, finely chopped
CHIVES	1 teaspoon, finely chopped
MILK	2 cups

Melt BUTTER in a saucepan, stir in FLOUR and cook 1 minute. Stir in the next 5 ingredients and slowly add the MILK, stirring constantly, until thickened. Serve over vegetables or with fish or chicken loaf. Makes 2 cups.

GRAPE SAUCE

GRAPE JUICE	1 cup
GRAPE JELLY	1/2 cup
POMEGRANATE JUICE	or cranberry juice, 1/2 cup
VINEGAR	2 tablespoons
CORNSTARCH	2 tablespoons
ONION JUICE	4 teaspoons

| GINGER | 1/4 teaspoon |
| MUSTARD | dry, 1/4 teaspoon |

Heat GRAPE JUICE and JELLY until JELLY is melted. Mix the POMEGRANATE JUICE and VINEGAR together and stir in the CORNSTARCH; add the remaining ingredients. Stir into the grape mixture and cook until thickened. Serve with pork, tongue or game birds. Makes about 2 cups.

HOLAN SAUCE

EGG YOLKS	4
WATER	1 tablespoon
BUTTER	2/3 cup, at room temperature
SALT	1/4 teaspoon
PEPPER	freshly ground, white
VINEGAR	tarragon, 1 tablespoon

Place EGG YOLKS and WATER in a small saucepan and beat with a whisk. Place pan over hot, not boiling, water over low heat. Beat until foamy. Beat in BUTTER piece by piece until all BUTTER has been added and sauce has thickened. Add SALT and PEPPER. Whisk in VINEGAR. (If sauce separates, just add 1 tablespoon boiling water and beat until smooth.) Makes 2 cups.

SAUCE MELITA

BUTTER	1/2 cup
FLOUR	3 tablespoons
WATER	2 cups
EGG YOLKS	3
CREAM	heavy, 2 tablespoons
VINEGAR	1 tablespoon
SALT	
PEPPER	freshly ground white

Melt 3 tablespoons BUTTER in a saucepan; stir in FLOUR and cook 1 minute. Add WATER and cook until smooth and thickened. Beat the EGG YOLKS with the CREAM and gradually stir in some of the hot mixture. Return to the saucepan; heat but do not boil. Add the VINEGAR and season to taste with SALT and PEPPER. Remove from heat and beat in the remaining BUTTER, 1 tablespoon at a time. Makes about 3 cups.

PISTACHIO SALAD DRESSING

SALT	1 teaspoon
PEPPER	freshly ground white, 1/4 teaspoon
VINEGAR	1/4 cup
OLIVE OIL	1/2 cup
GARLIC	1 clove, crushed
PISTACHIO NUTS	2 tablespoons, chopped

Combine ingredients in a jar and shake thoroughly. Serve with fruit salad, sea food or mixed greens. Makes about 3/4 cup.

ERECH DRESSING

Oil And Vinegar Dressing

SALT	1 teaspoon
PEPPER	freshly ground black or white, 1/4 teaspoon
OLIVE OIL	3/4 cup
VINEGAR	1/4 cup

Put ingredients in a small jar; cover and shake thoroughly. Onion juice may be added if desired. Makes 1 cup.

FRUIT SALAD DRESSING

OIL	3/4 cup
GRAPE JELLY	2 tablespoons
VINEGAR	white, 2 tablespoons
MUSTARD	dry, 1/2 tablespoon
SALT	1 teaspoon
GARLIC	1 medium clove, crushed

Combine all ingredients in a bottle and shake well or homogenize in a blender. Serve over mixed fruits or salad greens. Makes 1 cup.

ODDMENTS

JAVAN DRESSING
Egg and Oil Dressing (Mayonnaise)

MUSTARD	dry, 1 teaspoon
SALT	1 teaspoon
EGG YOLKS	2
VINEGAR	1/4 cup
OIL	2 cups

In a small bowl add MUSTARD, SALT and EGG YOLKS. Beat well with a whisk or rotary beater until well blended. Slowly add 2 tablespoons VINEGAR beating constantly. Add 1 cup OIL, 1 tablespoon at a time while continuing to beat. Add the remaining VINEGAR and OIL 1 tablespoon at a time. A blender may be used to make this dressing. Makes 2 cups.

PARSLEY SAUCE

PARSLEY	flat leaf, 1/2 cup
CAPERS	2 tablespoons
SOUR PICKLE	1 tablespoon, chopped
MUSTARD	dry, 1 tablespoon
SUGAR	1/2 teaspoon
SALT	1/2 teaspoon
PEPPER	1/4 teaspoon, freshly ground
GREEN ONIONS	2, coarsely chopped
JAVAN DRESSING	p. 183, or mayonnaise, 1 cup
GARLIC	1 clove, chopped
EGG	1, hard-cooked, chopped

Combine all ingredients in a blender and blend until smooth. Serve with fish, cold meats or hard-cooked eggs. Makes about 1 1/4 cups.

ROMAN TOPPING

BUTTER	1/3 cup, softened
SUGAR	1 cup
ROSEWATER	or lemon extract, 1 teaspoon

Cream BUTTER; add SUGAR a little at a time, beating after each addition. Add flavoring a few drops at a time. Chill. Serve on puddings. Makes about 1 cup.

EGGNOG SAUCE

EGGS	2, separated, at room temperature
SUGAR	1/2 cup
SALT	1/8 teaspoon
CREAM	heavy, 1 cup
ALMOND EXTRACT	1/8 teaspoon
NUTMEG	ground

Beat EGG yolks until thick and lemon colored; add 1/4 cup SUGAR gradually and beat well. Beat EGG whites until stiff and gradually beat in remaining 1/4 cup SUGAR and the SALT. Fold into the EGG yolk mixture. Whip the CREAM until stiff and add ALMOND EXTRACT and fold into the combined EGG mixture. Chill. Sprinkle with NUTMEG before serving. Serve on cake or bread pudding. Makes about 3 cups.

BEREA DRESSING

Grenadine Cream Dressing

VINEGAR	4 teaspoons
SALT	1/4 teaspoon
GRENADINE SYRUP	1/4 cup
CREAM	heavy, 1/2 cup, whipped

Stir VINEGAR and SALT into the GRENADINE SYRUP

and slowly add the whipped CREAM. Serve over fruit salads. Makes about 1 1/4 cups.

GRENADINE SYRUP

POMEGRANATES ripe
SUGAR

Remove pulp from POMEGRANATES. Measure equal amounts of SUGAR and pulp, mix together and let stand for 24 hours. Bring to a boil and immediately strain through a sieve. Do not bruise the seeds. Pour the syrup into sterilized jars and seal.

CINNAMON SYRUP

WATER	2 cups
CINNAMON BARK	one 2 inch piece, crushed
SUGAR	1/3 cup

Pour 2 cups of boiling water over the CINNAMON BARK; let steep for 1 hour. Add SUGAR and boil 5 minutes. For sauces and drinks.

POMEGRANATE SYRUP

POMEGRANATES 6, peeled
SUGAR

Remove white part of POMEGRANATES after peeling. Press the seeds and squeeze the juice through a cloth. For each pint of juice add 10 ounces of SUGAR and simmer 10 minutes. Skim and put into bottles. For sauces and drinks.

FOR THOSE WHO THIRST

Ho, everyone that thirsteth . . .
ISAIAH 55:1

In summertime, the pink pulp of watermelons and other fruits was crushed and mixed with water to quench the thirst and gladden the heart. Various fruit drinks were enjoyed by biblical people. Since sugar cane did not grow in the Holy Land, but had to be imported, it was a luxury of the rich. And so honey was combined with the juice of apricots, quince and grapes to make a sweet syrup used as a flavoring or mixed with water to make a fruit punch. The grenadine we use today was prepared in this way from the juice of the pomegranate.

Many flavorful drinks were made from steeped herbs and spices which grew easily in the sun-drenched area. They were used fresh or dried and many were found to have medicinal qualities. Spring flowers, too, were stripped of their petals to make a fragrant beverage. To this day fragrant teas made from plants and vegetables are enjoyed.

In a country where water was scarce and carefully rationed, beverages played an important part at all meals and special feasts. The word "feast" itself comes from the Hebrew and Greek verbs "to drink."

In all, the grape vine is mentioned more than 200 times in the Bible. And today we know that several of the psalms began as ancient songs, composed to celebrate the grape harvest and pass the time while the juice was being pressed from the grapes.

Grown on terraced hills, grapes were first gathered in late summer and their harvest lasted almost six weeks, until well into October. This long season of grape gathering and pressing was the Israelites' most joyous holiday of thanksgiving, and was celebrated in fine style, with much singing and feasting and dancing. Everywhere ripened grapes, often the size of small plums, were cut from the vine in large clusters (some weighing more than 20 pounds), and then gathered into baskets.

Most of the fruit found its way into the presses. The grapes were either spread out for a few days to let their sugars increase, or heaped at once into the presses located right in the vineyard, as pictured in Isaiah:

> My well-beloved hath a vineyard in a very fruitful hill: And he fenced it, and gathered out the stones thereof and planted it with the choicest vine, and built a tower in the midst of it, and also made a winepress therein.
>
> Isaiah: 5:1, 2

The fresh grapes were trod by foot into a sweet grape juice which flowed from the press through an open channel into a vat. The tart juice of the green grape was used, just as we use lemon juice and vinegar today. It is both a food preserver and a beverage when diluted with water.

All around the world Christians and Jews use juice from the grape to celebrate their most important religious events.

APRICOT FROTH

EGG	1
APRICOT JUICE	1 cup
MILK	1 cup
ALMOND EXTRACT	1/8 teaspoon
HONEY	2 tablespoons

Put all ingredients into a blender or beat EGG until light and fluffy and put into a glass jar with the remaining ingredients and shake well. Makes 2 drinks.

ROSE OF SHARON

POMEGRANATE JUICE or cranberry juice, 3 cups
WATER 1 cup
ROSE WATER 1/4 cup
HONEY or sugar
GRENADINE SYRUP

Mix the first 3 ingredients together and add HONEY to taste. Pour into a refrigerator tray and freeze until almost firm. Empty into a bowl; beat with a whisk until mushy and return to the tray. Freeze until firm. Break up with a fork and divide between four 6 ounce glasses. Pour over 1 tablespoon or more of GRENADINE SYRUP for each glass.

MINT JULEP

MINT JELLY 1/4 to 1/2 cup
MILK 2 cups
MINT LEAVES fresh, 2 large sprigs

Put MINT JELLY and MILK in a blender or shake well in a glass jar. Garnish each glass with the fresh MINT. Makes 2 drinks.

FESTIVAL EGGLESS NOG

MILK 1 quart
POMEGRANATE JUICE or cranberry juice, 1 1/2 cups
GRENADINE SYRUP 1/2 cup
HONEY 5 tablespoons

Put all ingredients in a blender or shake well in a glass jar. Makes 6 drinks.

ELISHA'S DRINK

Hot Carob Cup

CAROB POWDER or cocoa, 1/2 cup
HONEY 6 tablespoons

SALT	1/8 teaspoon
MILK	6 cups, scalded
CREAM	heavy, 1 cup whipped
CINNAMON	ground

Combine the first 3 ingredients in a saucepan. Stir in a little scalded MILK to make a smooth paste; add remaining MILK. With a wire whisk, over low heat, beat for 1 minute or until very frothy and hot. Pour into mugs and float CREAM on top. Dust with CINNAMON. Makes 6 cups.

WANDERER'S JOY

Yogurt Drink

WATER	2 cups
SALT	1/8 teaspoon
YOGURT	2 cups
MINT	4 large sprigs, optional

Beat cold WATER and SALT into the YOGURT until well blended; chill. Garnish with MINT. Serves 4.

HERB TEAS

Herb teas or infusions made from either fresh or dried herbs are a welcome change from leaf tea and are brewed in the same way. A china, glass or earthenware pot, preheated by rinsing with boiling water, is the first requirement. One teaspoon of dried herbs for each cup and one for the pot or one tablespoon of fresh leaves per cup is the average strength. Some herbs become bitter if steeped too long. Cold water is brought to a boil and poured directly over the leaves, which have been put into the heated pot, and allowed to steep for 5 to 10 minutes.

The following are herbs frequently used for making tea:

Anise	Cumin	Marjoram
Caraway	Dandelion	Mint
Camomile	Fennel	Parsley
Coriander	Hyssop	Thyme

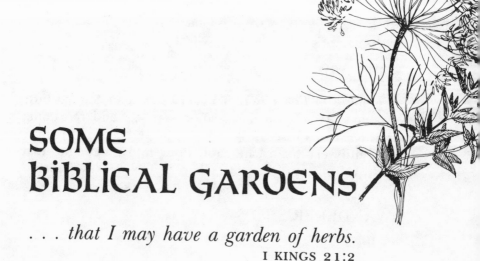

SOME
BiBLICAL GARDENS

. . . that I may have a garden of herbs.
I KINGS 21:2

The most ancient gardens were herb gardens. Herbs, since the dawn of time, have been highly valued for medicines, for flavoring foods, for fragrance, and for beauty. Trading in herbs was also a way to great wealth and trade caravans on their way to Egypt, Greece, and Rome jealously guarded the secret locations of their spices and herbs from the Far East. Twenty centuries before Christ's birth, these traders enter the Bible when Joseph's brothers sell him to "a company of Ishmaelites [who] came from Gilead with their camels bearing spicery and balm and myrrh, going to carry it down to Egypt" (Genesis 37:25).

Today, families, groups, or individuals who plant biblical gardens will find many rewards. The colors of herbs are subtle and muted from olive to blue to gray, and their leaves give a cool and inviting look to summer gardens and bouquets. Because many are perennials, herbs do not need yearly replenishing. They must be cut back to encourage fullness and to control growth; all clippings unwanted for cooking yield their fragrance when burned in the fireplace. Herbs unused for fresh seasoning of summer foods may be dried or frozen for winter use. Each herb has not only an economic, culinary, and aesthetic use, but each is rich in history.

SOME BIBLICAL GARDENS

THE PLANTS

ANISE
(Pimpenella Anisum)

> *Woe unto you, scribes and Pharisees, hypocrites! for ye pay tithe of mint and anise and cummin, and have omitted the weightier matters of the law, judgment, mercy and faith: these ought ye to have done, and not to leave the other undone.*
>
> *Matthew 23:23*

Thus Jesus rebuked the Pharisees for their outward and obvious pretense of religion. All modern scholars agree that the word should not have been translated as *anise,* but that it should be "mint and *dill* and cumin."

Anise, the licorice-flavored herb, was a favorite in ancient Roman cooking. Kings perfumed their linen with the herb. Later, during the plagues of the middle ages, anise was used as a disinfectant. It has been used to cure indigestion and to sweeten breath. Not only used in cakes, breads, and teas, anise may be chopped to flavor sauces and salads.

Anise is an annual which grows eighteen inches high. It may be sewn directly into rich and well-drained soil in a sunny location during May. Six weeks later when the seed heads are grayish, it may be harvested.

CARAWAY
(Carvum Carvi)

The caraway seed dates back to the first century A.D. when it was used as a medicine in treating various diseases. It is believed to have taken its name from the province of Caria in the Middle East and to have been brought to Egypt by spice traders. The seed is used worldwide in everything from soups to desserts. The leaves are boiled as potherbs; the roots are sweet and reminiscent of a parsnip. Oil was extracted from the seeds and used in flavoring medicines, beverages and food.

Caraway is a biennial and may be sown in early autumn or spring. It grows eight inches the first year but does not come to seed until the second year. Because of the tap root, caraway should be planted in the garden in a location where it will remain. For indoor planting, sow two or three seeds to a pot and remove all but the strongest seedling. When ready to transplant, remove and plant with care. Caraway can also be started in peat pots and then placed directly into the garden soil. It grows to two feet in height and should be covered for winter protection.

CORIANDER
(Coriander Sativum)

> And the house of Israel called the name thereof Manna: and it was like coriander seed, white.
>
> *Exodus 16:31*

One of the "bitter herbs" of Passover, coriander grew in the Hanging Gardens of Babylon and is mentioned as a medical plant in use in Thebes. Coriander smells similar to tangy orange peel, and it was used in medicine as flavoring. One of the major ingredients of curry seasoning, coriander also adds flavor to breads, cakes, meats, and fish.

Coriander is an annual which is slow to germinate. It may be sewn in fall as well as spring in dry, light soil, four to five inches apart. Seedheads ripen in midsummer; they should be picked before they fall to the ground and re-seed themselves. Coriander grows one to two feet tall with white and pink-tinged flowers. It can be cut back and makes an attractive house plant.

CUMIN
(Cuminum Cyminum)

> For the fitches are not threshed with a threshing instrument, neither is a cartwheel turned about upon the cummin: but the fitches are beaten out with a staff, and the cummin with a rod.
>
> *Isaiah 28:27*

Thus Isaiah promised that God would not be too severe in punishing His straying people; he would not crush them as grain is crushed. Cumin is again mentioned in Matthew as part of the tithe. Cumin is native to Turkey, Egypt and Syria; it was probably introduced by Solomon into Israel. Cumin was ground and spread on bread; it was a substitute for pepper and is still an ingredient in curries. It was used medicinally as a poultice for eyes and blended for perfume.

Cumin is an annual and prefers a well-drained, sunny location. Seedlings should be thinned to eight inches apart. Seeds mature in July when they may be picked and dried. Bearing small white or rose flowers, cumin reaches a height of one foot.

SOME BiBLiCAL GARDENS

DILL
(Anethum graveolens)

Dill was not mentioned by name in the Bible, but various translators believe that the reference to anise in Matthew 23:23 should have been dill. Dill is used for pickling, for seasoning, and in vinegars.

Through the ages there have been many conflicting superstitions about dill. Some thought that witches and sorcerers used the seed to cast spells and others hung bunches of dill over the doorway to protect the house from evil. The Romans cut the flowery dill to adorn their heads during festivals. Ladies of the court used dill and rosewater for their complexions. As another aid to beauty, they brewed the leaves and seeds in a broth they drank to help them stay thin.

Dill grows two to three feet tall and prefers a sunny location.

FENNEL
(Foeniculum Officinalis)

Fennel was given as a reward to the famous runner Pheidippides in 500 BC when he alerted the Greeks to the Persian invasion of their shores. Ever since he has been depicted in paintings and statuary holding a sprig of fennel, and winning athletes thereafter wore fennel as a crown of victory. On festival occasions garlands of fennel were woven and carried by young girls in the various processionals. It was extensively used in medicine and through the ages there are many references to its being beneficial to fading eyesight.

Fennel is a perennial growing to four feet or over in height and flowering in July and August. It makes a desirable plant for the background of a perennial garden. The leaves and seeds have an anise-like flavor and the bulb is reminiscent of licorice. The bulbous bottom of the plant may be substituted in any recipe calling for celery either raw or cooked. The ground seeds are used in bread, cake and cookies and the whole seeds, when brewed, make a flavorful tea.

Fennel seeds should be planted in early spring after danger of frost is past. Soil must be spaded deeply and seeds sown one fourth inch deep in rows twelve inches apart; they germinate in fourteen to eighteen days and should be thinned to eight inches apart. Plants may be started indoors and successfully transplanted; they may be propagated by dividing the roots. The seeds should be harvested before they are fully ripe.

biblical garden cookery

FLAX
(Linum Usitatissimum)

> *She seeketh wool, and flax, and worketh willingly with her hands.*
>
> Proverbs 31:13

The good wife of Proverbs, as all women of biblical times, wove linen from one of the earliest textile fibers cultivated in Egypt and Palestine. Stalks of flax were laid on the flat roofs to dry and bleach in the hot sun. The flax was then spun and woven into hangings and curtains for the Tabernacle and for priestly garments: "And the priest shall put on his linen garment, and his linen breeches" (Leviticus 6:10). The linen was of varying quality, ranging from coarse to the finest: "And to her was granted that she should be arrayed in fine linen, clean and white, for the fine linen is the righteousness of saints" (Revelations 19:8). Fine linen was used as a burial cloth: "Then took they the body of Jesus, and wound it in linen clothes with the spices" (John 19:40).

Valued most for its fiber and for linseed oil, flax seed was also used in poultices and liniments. The remaining fiber was used for cattle feed. Flax seed has no distinct flavor; when toasted and browned it is used only for texture and food value in breads and cakes.

Flax blooms abundantly until frost, and its delicate blue flowers are an asset to any garden. Grown in ordinary soil and germinating in three to four weeks, flax grows to two feet in height.

HYSSOP
(Hyssopus Officinalis)

> *Purge me with hyssop, and I shall be clean: wash me, and I shall be whiter than snow.*
>
> Psalm 51:7

> *Now there was set a vessel full of vinegar: and they filled a sponge with vinegar, and put it upon hyssop and put it to his mouth.*
>
> John 19:29

Although much has been written about hyssop, few scholars agree on which plant was used to wet the lips of Jesus. There are more than a dozen suggestions, among them rue, marjoram and summer savory. According to Jewish ritual law, that which was defiled had to be purified by sprinkling water from a bunch of hyssop. The hyssop used in today's gardens belongs to the mint family.

The tops of hyssop flowers can be used to flavor soups and salads and to make a refreshing tea. Oil from hyssop is used to make eau de cologne.

An attractive evergreen plant for edging, hyssop flowers are usually blue, though rarer varieties are pink or white. Hyssop tolerates shade; it must be winter protected and replaced every three to four years.

MINT
(Mentha Longifolia)

There are more than forty varieties of mint, which was one of the "bitter herbs" of the Bible. The Pharisees paid their tithe with the so-called horse mint. The leaves were used in flavoring drinks and foods and the extracted oil was an ingredient in soap and medical preparations. The aromatic herb was strewn on the floor of the temples and infused for the infrequent baths which were considered a great luxury. Chewing the leaves was believed to eradicate various ailments of the intestinal tract.

Mint may be grown from seed but the plant multiplies rapidly if started from root division. Since mint has strong nomadic tendencies, plants must be restricted by tin strips, bricks or slate to keep them from taking over the garden. Mint thrives in either full sun or partial shade and prefers a not-too-rich soil. It reaches two feet in height outdoors, but may be grown indoors as a house plant if kept cut back to about one foot in height.

The lemon or apple flavored mints are particularly desirable varieties to include in the garden or as a house plant.

MUSTARD
(Brassica, Alba)

> *If ye have faith as a grain of mustard seed ye shall say unto this mountain, Remove hence to yonder place; and it shall remove; and nothing shall be impossible unto you.*
>
> *Matthew 17:20*

> *It is like a grain of mustard seed, which, when it is sown in the earth is less than all the seeds that be in the earth: But when it is sown, it groweth up, and becometh greater than all herbs, and shooteth out great branches, so that the fowls of the air may lodge under the shadow of it.*
>
> *Mark 4:31–32*

Like the tiny mustard seed, once the Gospel is planted, it will grow and fill the earth. Mustard spreads quickly and must be controlled in the garden. Mustard seeds have a piquant taste only when crushed and a liquid is added. Mustard is an ancient and valued herb; the Chinese have known it for thousands of years and Roman soldiers carried it with them into battle.

Mustard is used for meats, but it also flavors sweets, including gingerbread. The old-fashioned and dreaded mustard plaster is one example of its use in medicine.

The feathery mustard plant is an annual which grows three feet high with pale yellow, four petaled flowers. The green leaves, when young, may be used for salads. When the tiny seedheads are ripe, the seeds can be harvested and stored.

PARSLEY
(Petroselinum Crispum)

Parsley grew wild and abundantly in Bibleland and was one of the first herbs to be cultivated. Like fennel, it was a sign of victory and achievement and the ancient Roman athletes wore crowns woven of this herb. St. Paul refers to this "corruptible crown" (I Corinthians 9:25).

Many superstitions surround this dark green, curly plant. Funeral wreaths were fashioned out of it to decorate graves. Considered a valuable herb in medicine, it was used in the treatment of stomach disorders. Today we use the versatile plant as an ingredient in many dishes and as a garnish to beautify platters.

This biennial belongs to the carrot family; because it has a tap root, it should be started in small pots, two or three seeds to a pot. Only the strongest shoot should be kept and the others pulled out. Parsley should be started indoors because of slow germination; it takes from one month to six weeks to appear. To hasten germination, soak seeds twenty-four hours in water before planting them. Parsley makes an attractive edging for a vegetable garden and grows about one foot high.

RUE
(Ruta Graveolens)

> *for ye tithe mint and rue and all manner of herbs . . .*
> *Luke 11:42*

SOME BibLical GARDENS

One of the bitter herbs, rue was used as a disinfectant and for medicinal magic. It was supposed to have provided protection against germs in time of plague.

Rue is an ingredient for potpourri. Used sparingly, it adds an interesting flavor to meats and vegetables. Rue has yellow flowers, grows two to three feet high, and likes a moist, well-drained soil. Rue is a lovely, lacy blue-green plant, which can be used attractively to edge a garden. When dried, its seed heads resemble bells and may be gilded for wreaths.

SAFFRON
(Crocus Sativus)

Solomon sang the praises of saffron brought to him over the trade routes from Egypt. It was valued for its color, fragrance and flavor. This small crocus produced the orange-scarlet stigmas used in medicine and dyes. The crocus bulb or corms proved fatal if eaten raw, but Egyptian women sliced and boiled and served them with no ill effects. However, the saffron threads were considered a great addition to the flavoring in salads, sauces and sweetmeats. As late as the fifteenth century A.D., the corms were strung around the necks of the wary to ward off ailments and its infusions bathed the eyes and sores of the afflicted. The powder from the stigma was used for tea and the oil extracted from the herb was burned with frankincense. Saffron was used lavishly for perfuming amphitheaters, temples and other public places. It took thousands of flowers to produce one pound of commercial saffron. Over the years the flowers have become less plentiful and the price of saffron has soared.

Saffron may be planted from seed or from the bulb. If planted in September in a well sheltered sandy soil only the foliage will appear in May. By fall the little three inch lavender flowers will bloom.

These mild, violet, scented flowers should be picked when first opened for harvesting and the stigma pinched off with the finger tips and dried in the sun or slowly in the oven. The corms should be divided every three or four years for continuing bloom.

SAGE
(Salvia Officinalis)

Sage comes from the Latin word *salvere,* "to be well and to save." It was believed that sage would brighten dimming eyesight, prevent depression,

197

prolong life and fight off the ravages of old age. There is an ancient Arabian saying, "How can a man die with sage in his garden?"

The young also benefited from this wondrous herb. Around their necks babies often wore twelve leaves of sage, denoting the twelve Apostles, to lessen the discomfort of teething. The plant was the inspiration of artisans for the seven branched candlestick. The branches, when laid flat, formed a design that has been a symbol in religion for centuries. Sage, a versatile herb, can be brewed into tea, used as a gargle and added to many foods to enhance the flavor.

Sage likes a sunny spot in a well drained soil. It needs little care and lasts for several years. Over watering and mites are the worst enemies. If sign of mites appears, bathe the leaves with a mixture of one tablespoon dishwashing detergent and one pint of water every month. Plants may be started from seeds or cuttings in early summer. The seeds take about two weeks to germinate. Pinch tops to encourage bushy plants. Mulch to protect from thaws and freezing. Sage grows two to four feet high depending on sun and soil. For indoor growing, cut the plant back to ten inches. Because of its woody structure, sage may be cut into topiary form or made into bonsai. The gray-green leaves of sage are long and oval with a pebbly texture; the flowers appear in June with masses of purplish blossoms, much to the delight of the bees.

SUMMER SAVORY
(Satureia Hortensis)

Summer savory is an annual herb a foot in height, native to the Mediterranean region; it belongs to the mint family. Winter savory is a woody, spreading variety which is very similar in taste but considered not as desirable in flavor for cooking. The savories were known in Biblical times by the Greek name *isope* or hyssop which has led to much misunderstanding in identifying the plants. The sharp, spicy-flavored green leaf of summer savory is an addition to almost every food from fruit to stews. Because of its great affinity for fresh and dried beans, it is commonly known as the "bean herb."

SWEET MARJORAM
(Origanum Majorana)

Sweet marjoram, wild marjoram and pot marjoram are the three varieties of the marjoram species that have survived through the years. Originally there were more than thirty varieties of this interesting herb. Because of the plant's medicinal properties and unique flavor, nomads carried it from the Orient and India. It is now indigenous to all parts of the world.

Sweet marjoram was the symbol of romantic love. It was strewn on the floors of monasteries and manor halls for festival and holy occasions. Pliny, Virgil and other Roman writers mentioned the herb often; in Greek mythology, Venus was credited as the first to cultivate marjoram. The horticultural name *origanum* means "joy of the mountain." In different countries, the plant had various meanings. In India it was a sacred herb and in the Orient it was believed to have the power to dispel sorrow. This aromatic herb has been closely associated with food. The oil from the plant was an ingredient in perfume, lotions, soap and other cosmetics.

Marjoram is an annual which grows eight to twelve inches tall.

THYME
(Thyme Vulgaris)

Thyme was often referred to as the herb of courage and happiness and was cultivated in Biblical days chiefly for attracting bees in order to produce a superior flavored honey. Thyme thrived in areas where goats and sheep grazed; their meat was permeated with the pungent flavor. The word *thyme* means incense, for it was mixed with other sweet smelling substances to burn in the lamps.

Because it was planted on graves to give everlasting fragrance it was known as the funeral plant. The oil from the flowers was used in ointments, antiseptics, soap and cosmetics and to flavor drinks and foods.

One of the favorites of the twenty-eight varieties of thyme is citriodorus which is lemon scented. It is a recumbent plant which flowers in late June with pale lavender blossoms and is one of the hardiest of the family. Another thyme, azoricus, with the flavor of tangerine-orange, can be mixed with the lemon flavored thyme for an unusual taste in desserts and herb teas.

Seeds should be planted in flats in early spring and transplanted to the garden after danger of frost is past. Thyme is suitable for an edging or planting among rocks. Although it is a perennial, it should be renewed every three to four years.

WORMWOOD
(Artemisca Absinthum)

And the angel sounded, and there fell a great star from heaven burning as

it was a lamp, and it fell upon the third part of the rivers, and upon the
fountains of waters; and the name of the star is called Wormwood: and the
third part of the waters became wormwood; and many men died of the
waters, because they were made bitter.

Revelation 8:10–11

"Gall and wormwood" are signs of punishment and suffering. This bitter herb as part of a liniment can be used for healing, but it has also been an agent of slow death.

Wormwood has little culinary value because it is so bitter. It may be used in small quantites to flavor cheese and cakes. But it does give an aromatic fragrance to the garden. Wormwood, a member of the aster family, has silvery leaves and grows twelve to fourteen inches high. It spreads quickly, and must be clipped often for border use.

THE GARDENS

Biblical herbs thrive in the sun with good drainage. They may be planted between rows in a vegetable garden, grown along walks, arranged in clumps in front of shrubs or mixed in borders with flowers and bulbs. Herbs flourish in a tiny plot by the kitchen door, in a narrow sunny strip, or in pots on a terrace. Or they may be patterned into the lovely knot gardens which trace their history from medieval times to the present. Wherever they are planted, the addition of flowers native to the Holy Land, such as lupin, chrysanthemum, tulip, narcissus or anemone, creates a harmonious garden.

Indoor gardens are for those without outdoor space or for those who like to bring herbs indoors for the winter. An indoor window box lined with tin is ideal, for individual pots can be sunk into peat moss to be kept moist. For those without window boxes, herbs may be grouped dramatically by setting pots in rows at different heights. All indoor herbs should have direct sunlight each day. They may be interspersed with flowering plants for more color.

SEEDTIME

Biblical gardens may be started indoors in peat pots. In moist (not soggy) and sterile soil, six seeds can be pressed gently into each pot. The pots

SOME BIBLICAL GARDENS

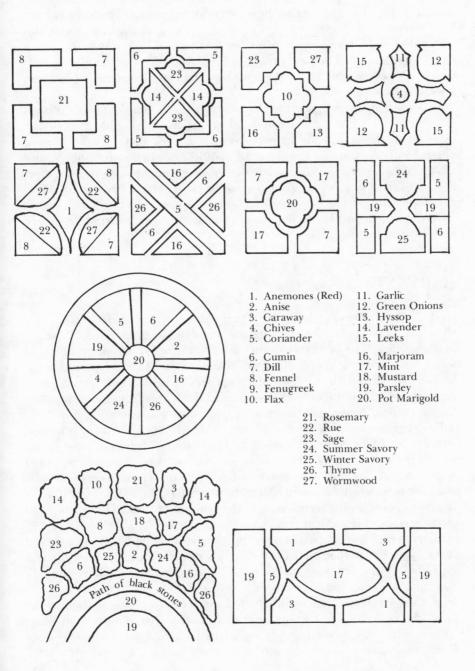

1. Anemones (Red)
2. Anise
3. Caraway
4. Chives
5. Coriander

6. Cumin
7. Dill
8. Fennel
9. Fenugreek
10. Flax

11. Garlic
12. Green Onions
13. Hyssop
14. Lavender
15. Leeks

16. Marjoram
17. Mint
18. Mustard
19. Parsley
20. Pot Marigold

21. Rosemary
22. Rue
23. Sage
24. Summer Savory
25. Winter Savory
26. Thyme
27. Wormwood

should be kept out of direct sunlight, in room temperature between 60 and 70 degrees, and moistened gently. Most herbs germinate in about two weeks, but some take longer. After the first pair of leaves appears, plants should be thinned. The peat pots may be placed directly into 3″ clay pots with more potting soil; after the plants have six leaves they may be fed with a weak solution of plant food.

For outdoor planting, seedlings must be gradually "hardened off." Placed outdoors in the shade for a couple of hours, plants should gradually be exposed to direct sun for several days. In a week they may be planted permanently in a sunny location but should be watched for wilting and shaded if necessary. Seeds may also be planted directly into the soil after danger of frost passes; the soil must not be permitted to become hard and dry, especially during germination. When they are six inches tall, plants should be pinched back to encourage bushier growth for wind resistance and appearance.

HARVEST

Herbs, after harvesting, may be preserved by drying or freezing. They should be harvested in the morning after the dew has evaporated. Rinse the herbs gently and suspend them to dry in a place protected from sunlight and with good air circulation. Within two weeks, they should be crisp. Leaf herbs may also be dried in the oven on a baking sheet with the lowest possible heat and the oven door open. After drying, strip the leaves from the stem; store them in a dry, airtight container away from heat and strong light.

Herbs grown for their seeds may also be dried. When the plant is tapped and the seed falls easily, it is ripe and ready to be harvested. Seed heads should then be removed, placed between two pieces of cloth, and pounded with a stick. As in the age-old practice of winnowing, a light breeze will blow away the near weightless chaff. After the seeds have been left a few days to dry on a cheesecloth-covered screen, they should be packed in dry, airtight containers away from heat and light.

Many prefer the modern convenience of freezing herbs. Leaves should remain attached to their stems and then tied in small bunches. After blanching in boiling water for one minute, the bunch should be plunged immediately into ice water for two to three minutes. Leaves may then be removed from their stems and placed in labelled freezer bags. Some herbs such as basil, chives and dill need only be washed and frozen without blanching. Although the frozen herbs should be defrosted before being added to cold foods, they may be added directly to cooking foods.

SOME BIBLICAL GARDENS

They will lose some of their flavor if subjected to lengthy cooking. Herb seasoning for soups, for example, should be tied in cheesecloth and added only during the last half hour of cooking. The flavor of a sauce or butter is enhanced if the herbs are added and allowed to set half an hour before reheating and serving.

Fresh leaf herbs should be finely chopped or blended. The greatest amount of exposed surface will release the most oils. Seeds from herbs should be ground in as small a quantity as needed at the time; a special pepper mill may be kept for seed herbs only.

The planting, growing, and enjoyment of herbs is deeply satisfying, and it is also a spiritual link with biblical history.

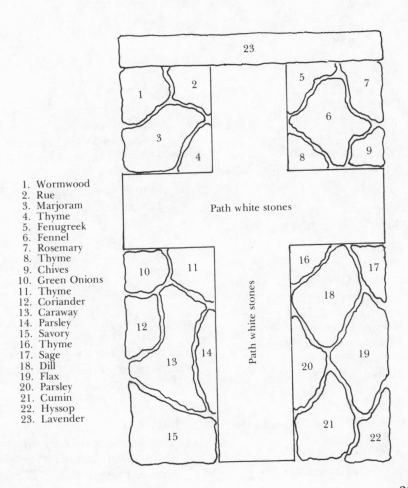

1. Wormwood
2. Rue
3. Marjoram
4. Thyme
5. Fenugreek
6. Fennel
7. Rosemary
8. Thyme
9. Chives
10. Green Onions
11. Thyme
12. Coriander
13. Caraway
14. Parsley
15. Savory
16. Thyme
17. Sage
18. Dill
19. Flax
20. Parsley
21. Cumin
22. Hyssop
23. Lavender

iNDEX

ALMONDS
  history of 30
  Almond Cheese Dessert 100
  Almond Cream 99
  Cream of Almond Soup Adoraim
    13

ANISE
  history and gardening 191

APPETIZERS
  cheese
    Black Olive and Cheese Savory
      3
    Cheese and Anchovy Spread 2
    Fried Cheese 3
    Radish Cheese Spread 2
    Roquefort Coins 1
    Shepherd's Spread 3
    Watercress Spread 2
  fruit
    Broiled Fresh Figs and Dates 7
    Fruit Fritters 6
  meat, fish, and egg
    Cilicia Cucumbers 11

Esther's Appetizers with Onion
    and Meat Filling 5
  Euphrates Pickled Herring 9
  Hebron Chicken Liver and Egg
    Spread 4
  Minted Lamb Nuggets 12
  Potted Tongue 4
  Seabobs 12
  Stuffed Eggs Cyrene 9
  Stuffed Grape Leaves 7
vegetables
  Bulgur and Mint Salad 11
  Cucumbers with Walnut Dress-
    ing 4
  Flavored Butters 8
  Stuffed Thistle Bottoms 66
  Tender Thistles (Stuffed Arti-
    choke Leaves) 10

APRICOTS
  history of 26
  Abigail's Apricot Whip 31
  Apricot Date Stuffing 173
  Apricot Froth 187

iNDEX

Apricot Nut Bread 87
Apricot Tarts 110
Forbidden Fruit Jam 43
Fruit Fritters Appetizer 6
Golden Apple Conserve 40
Lebanon Lamb with Apricots 150

ARTICHOKES
history of 49
Capernaum Thistles Stuffed with
        Chicken 54
Roman Spears 54
Stuffed Thistle Bottoms 66

BARLEY
history of 47
Barley Soup 18
Bethlehem Barley and Onions 91
Daybreak Bread 76
Palestine Four Flour Bread 79
Sour Milk and Barley Bread 76

BASS
Bass Galilee with Oyster Stuffing
        120

BEANS
history of 46
Adam's Stew (Lamb and Bean
        Casserole) 151
Antioch Salad 64

BEEF
history of 161
Basic Beef Stock 22
Braised Beef 164
Braised Short Ribs of Beef
        Goshen 164
Braised Steak Samuel 162
Broiled Skewered Spiced Beef 168
Honey Glazed Corned Beef 165
Meat Loaf Masada 163
Philippi Stuffed Flank Steak 162

BEVERAGES
history of 186–187
Apricot Froth 187
Elisha's (Hot Carob) Drink 188
Festival Eggless Nog 188
Herb Teas 189
Mint Julep 188
Rose of Sharon 188
Wanderer's Joy (Yogurt Drink)
        189

BRAINS
Brains Nicopolis with Curried
        Javan Dressing 176

BREADS, LEAVENED
history of 69–74
Bread with Whey 77
David's Rescue 85
Daybreak Bread 76
Ezekiel's Many-floured Bread
        81
Honeyed Griddle Cakes 78
Leavened Bread 84
Naomi's Little Breads 75
Palestine Four Flour Bread 79
Rebekah's Griddle Breads 80
Ruth's Journey Bread 74
Seed Bread 80
Sinai Herb Bread 82
Sour Milk and Barley Bread 76
Spiced Bread Galatia 83
Thessalonica Onion Bread 83
Unkneaded Bread of Thrace
        78

BREADS, SWEET
history of 72
Apricot Nut Bread 87
Date Nut Bread 89
Herdsman's Cake 87
Tea Bread Phenice 89

biblical garden cookery

BREADS, UNLEAVENED
history of 72
Caesarea Thins 86
Golan Discs 86

BUCKWHEAT GROATS
Firmity (Joseph's Gift to Benjamin) 91
Groats Herod with Veal Mariamne 166

BULGUR
Bulgur and Mint Salad 11

BUTTERS, FLAVORED
Walnut Butter 8
Watercress Butter 8

BUTTERMILK
Buttermilk Pancakes 90
Dessert Buttermilk Fries 98

CAKES
Fragrant Spice Cake 113
Fresh Fruit Cake 37
Herdsman's Cake 87
St. John's Chocolate Cake 103
Honey Cake from Egypt 107
Yogurt Cake 102
fillings
Sour Cream Filling 103
frostings and toppings
Eggnog Sauce 184
Dessert Cream 115
Honey Frosting 102
Roman Topping 184
St. John's Chocolate Frosting 106

CANDIES
Carob Sweets 109
Honeyed Nuts 113

CANTALOUPE
history of 28
Cantaloupe Conserve 41
Minted Melons 33
Sarah's Melon Jam 36
Shrimp in Melon 127

CARAWAY
history and gardening 191

CAROB (CHOCOLATE)
history of 30
Carob Drops 112
Carob Sweets 109
Chocolate Bread Pudding 105
Chocolate Fish 106
Chocolate Squares 106
Elisha's (Hot Carob) Drink 188
Mary's Kisses 108
St. John's Chocolate Cake 103
St. John's Chocolate Frosting 106

CHEESE
appetizers
Black Olive and Cheese Savory 3
Cheese and Anchovy Spread 2
Fried Cheese 3
Radish Cheese Spread 2
Ramoth Marinated Cheese 113
Roquefort Coins 1
Watercress Spread 2
Cheese Souffle 96
Endive and Roquefort Platter 52
Roquefort Soup 14
Spinach in Cheese Sauce 57

CHICKEN
history of 140
whole
Braised Chicken 141
Chicken Gaza 143

INDEX

Chicken in Sour Cream 141
Chicken with Lamb Stuffing 142
breasts
  Chicken with Mint and Herb Sauce 143
ground
  Courtyard Salad 144
  Hebron Chicken Liver and Egg Spread 4
  Shushan Chicken Loaf 144
stock
  Basic Chicken Stock 23

CHOCOLATE
  see Carob

CHUTNEY
  Spiced Date Chutney 32

CLAMS
  Broiled Clams 126

COD (FISH)
  Baked Stuffed Fish Tigras 119
  Crisp Tidbits 122

CONSERVES
  see Preserves and Conserves

COOKIES
  Anna's Favorite Honey Strips 35
  Apricot Tarts 110
  Carob Drops 112
  Chocolate Fish 106
  Jam Gems 112
  Mary's Kisses 108
  Negev Sand Cookies 111
  Nineveh Nuggets 32
  Pistachio Cookies 111
  Raisin Nut Bars 38
  Seed Snaps 110
  Sour Cream Cookies 100

CORIANDER
  history and gardening 192

"CORN"
  history of 47
  "Corn" 93

COTTAGE CHEESE
  Almond Cheese Dessert 100
  Homemade Cottage Cheese 96
  Meringue Cheesecake 97

CRAB
  Grecian Crab 127

CUCUMBERS
  history of 45
  Calah Cucumbers 52
  Cilicia Cucumbers 11
  Cucumbers and Radishes in Mint Dressing 50
  Cucumbers with Walnut Dressing 4
  Hot Cucumbers in Sour Cream 62
  Pergamos Pickles 51
  Persian Cucumber and Yogurt Soup 15
  Sweet and Sour Pickled Cucumbers 50

CUMIN
  history and gardening 192

CURRY
  Breaded Curried Eggs 146
  Chaldeah (Vegetable) Curry 61
  Curried Javan Dressing 176
  Curry Sauce 147

DATE
  history of 27
  Broiled Fresh Figs and Dates Appetizer 7

Date Nut Bread 89
Fruit Fritters Appetizers 6
Scones of Seir 104
Spiced Date Chutney 32

DILL
history and gardening 193

DUCK
Ahasuerus' Favorite Duck 137
Duck Salamis 138
Duck Phenicia with Walnut
    Stuffing 136
Spit-Roasted Wild Ducks 137

EGGS
Breaded Curried Eggs 146
Eggnog Sauce 184
Ham and Egg Salad 153
Scrambled Eggs Tarragon 146
Sour Cream Cress Omelet 145

ENDIVE
history of 48
Endive and Roquefort Platter 52
Stuffed Endives Reuben 64

FENNEL
history and gardening 193
Baked Fennel Bulbs 52
Fennel Salad 57

FIGS
history of 26
Broiled Fresh Figs and Dates Ap-
    petizer 7
Fig Hermits 31
Pickled Smyrna Figs 41

FISH
history of 116–118

soups
    Creamy Chowder 22
    Perga Catch 21
    Scallop Soup Alexandria 18
see varieties

FLAX
history and gardening 194

FROG'S LEGS 122

GARLIC
history of 46

GOAT
history of 149
Goat Cheeses, see Cheeses

GOOSE
history of 133
Goose with Grape Stuffing 135
Roast Goose with Wheat Pilaf
    Stuffing 134

GRAPE
history of 186–187
Angel's Grape Souffle 39
Grape Jelly 43
Grape Sauce 180
Grape Ketchup 39
Goose with Grape Stuffing 135
Spiced Grapes 40

HADDOCK
Creamed Haddock 121
Baked Stuffed Fish Tigras 119

HAM
history of 172
Alexandria Meat Loaf 157
Ham and Egg Salad 153

INDEX

Ham and Spinach Casserole 158
Kale with Ham 51

HEARTS
Hearts Hauran with Apricot Date
Stuffing 173

HERRING
Euphrates Pickled Herring 9

HONEY
history of 95
Anna's Favorite Honey Strips
35
Honey Cake from Egypt 107
Honey Cinnamon Syrup 108
Honey Frosting 102
Honey Syrup 91
Honeyed Nuts 113
Milk and Honey Soup 15
Rose and Honey Syrup 115

HYSSOP
history and gardening 194

JELLY
see Conserves and Preserves

KALE
Kale with Ham 51

KIDNEYS
Timothy's Choice Veal Kidneys
175

LAMB AND MUTTON
history of 148
Abel's Lamb 151
Adam's Stew (Lamb and Bean
Casserole) 151

King Solomon's Poached Lamb
160
Lamb Casserole 152
Lamb Stuffing 142
Lebanon Lamb with Apricots 150
Minted Lamb Nuggets 12
Skewered Lamb 150
Stuffed Grape Leaves 7
Stuffed Lamb Breast 159

LEEK
history of 47
Leeks Romano 65
Leek Salad 55

LENTILS
history of 46
Bethany Beans 53
Chaldea (Vegetable) Curry 61
Esau's Lentil Pottage 19
Lentils and Olive Salad 65
Palestine Four Flour Bread 79
Red Lentils 66

LETTUCE
Braised Romaine 67

LIVER
history of 172
Baked Calf's Liver 177

LOBSTER
Lobster Salad 126
Seabobs 12
Stuffed Broiled Lobster 130

MARINADE
Kedar (Mint) Marinade 179

MILLET
history of 70
Millet Judea 93
Tarsus Pie with Sauce for Saul 92

biblical garden cookery

MINT
history and gardening 195
Minted Melons 33
Mint Julep 188
Kedar (Mint) Marinade 179

MUSSELS
Mussels in Sauce 130

MUSTARD
history and gardening 195

OLIVES
history of 29
Black Olive and Cheese Savory 3
Black Olive Soup of Magdala 16
Lentils and Olive Salad 65

ONION
history of 45
Baked Onions 56
Curried Onions 68
Esther's Appetizers with Onion
Filling 5
Green Onions in Parsley Sauce 56
Onion Soup Seleucia 17
Pickled Onions 59
Scalloped Onions 58
Thessalonica Onion Bread 83
Vegetables Carmel (Spinach and
Green Onions) 60

OYSTERS
Creamed Oysters 129
Oyster Stuffing 120
Patmos Oyster Stew 20

PANCAKES
Buttermilk Pancakes 90
Sour Cream Pancakes 90

PARSLEY
history and gardening 196

PARTRIDGE
history of 133
Partridge in a Skillet 138

PASTRIES
Cream Puffs with Cheese Pis-
tachio Filling 101
Esther's Appetizers with Onion
and Meat Filling 5
Puff Cakes 100
Scones of Seir 104

PHEASANT
Spit-Roasted Pheasant 139

PICKLES
see Conserves and Preserves

PISTACHIO
history of 30
Cheese Pistachio Filling 101
Leah's Pistachio Pudding 35
Pistachio Cookies 111
Pistachio Nut Souffle 36
Pistachio Salad Dressing 182

POMEGRANATE
history of 28
Ararat Compote 33
Pomegranate Syrup 185

PORK
history of 149
Hazor Roast 156
Fried Pigs' Feet 158
Ribs of Joppa 156
Veal and Pork Bake 168

PRESERVES AND CONSERVES
fruit
Cantaloupe Conserve 41
Forbidden Fruit Jam 43

iNDEX

Golden Apple Conserve 40
Grape Jelly 43
Pickled Smyrna Figs 41
Quince Pickle 42
Sarah's Melon Jam 36
Spiced Grapes 40
Watermelon Jam 42
vegetable
    Pergamos Pickles (Cucumbers)
      51
    Pickled Onions 59
    Sweet and Sour Pickled Cucum-
      bers 50

PRETZELS
    history of 74
    "Little Arms" Pretzels 88

PUDDINGS
    Chocolate Bread Pudding 105
    Eggnog Sauce for Bread Pudding
      184
    Roman Topping for Puddings
      184
    Leah's Pistachio Pudding 35
    Manna Pudding 34
    Nut Raisin Pudding 37
    Pots of Cream 115
    Zipporah's Meringue-topped
      Bread Pudding 108

QUAIL
    history of 132
    Broiled Quail for Desert Wander-
      ers 139

QUINCE
    history of 28
    Quince Pickle 42

RABBIT OR HARE
    history of 149
    Fried Rabbit 155
    Gedara Hare (Rabbit) 154

RADISH
    Cucumbers and Radishes in Mint
      Dressing 50
    Radish Cheese Spread 2
    Salad Gilgal 59
    Watercress and Radish Stuffing
      119

RUE
    history and gardening 196

SAFFRON
    history and gardening 197

SAGE
    history and gardening 197

SALAD DRESSINGS
    Berea (Fruit Salad) Dressing 184
    Erech Dressing (Oil and Vinegar)
      182
    Fruit Salad Dressing 182
    Javan Dressing (Mayonnaise) 183
    Pistachio Salad Dressing 182
    Walnut Dressing 4

SALADS
    Antioch Salad 64
    Courtyard (Chicken Walnut)
      Salad 144
    Fennel Salad 57
    Ham and Egg Salad 153
    Leek Salad 55
    Lentils and Olive Salad 65
    Lobster Salad 126
    Martha's Mixed Salad 62

Miriam's Spinach Salad 63
Salad Gilgal (Radish) 59
Spinach Bacon Salad 61

SALMON
Cilicia Cucumbers (Salmon Salad
Stuffing) 11

SAUCES
dessert
Berea (Grenadine Cream)
Dressing 184
Cinnamon Syrup 185
Dessert Cream 115
Eggnog Sauce 184
Fruit Salad Dressing 182
Grenadine Syrup 185
Honey Syrup 91
Pomegranate Syrup 185
Rose and Honey Syrup 115
meat, fish, and eggs
Caper Sauce 160
Chive Sauce 159
Curried Javan Dressing 176
Curry Sauce 147
Dill Sauce 10
Grape Sauce 180
Holan Sauce 181
Javan Dressing 183
Parsley Sauce 183
Sarah's Sauce 180
Sauce Melita 181
Sauce for Saul 92
Tarragon Sauce 180

SCALLOPS
Broiled Scallops and Shrimp on
Skewers 129
Seabobs 12
Scallop Soup Alexandria 18

SHAD ROE NAZARETH 123

SHRIMP
Broiled Scallops and Shrimps on
Skewers 129
Seabobs 12
Shrimp in Melon 127
Stuffed Broiled Shrimp 128

SOLE, FILLET OF
Cold Summer Platter 124
Crisp Tidbits 122

SOUFFLES
Angel's Grape Souffle 39
Cheese Souffle 96
Pistachio Nut Souffle 36
Souffle of Rachel 104

SOUPS
Barley Soup 18
Basic Beef Stock 22
Basic Chicken Stock 23
Black Olive Soup of Magdala 16
Cream of Almond Soup Adoraim
13
Cream of Watercress Dothan 14
Creamy Chowder 22
Cyprus Lentil Stew 20
Esau's Lentil Pottage 19
Kedish Summer Soup 16
Milk and Honey Soup 15
Onion Soup Seleucia 17
Oxtail Soup 17
Patmos Oyster Stew 20
Perga Catch 21
Persian Cucumber and Yogurt
Soup 15
Roquefort Soup 14
Scallop Soup Alexandria 18
Spring Soup 15

SPARERIBS
Ribs of Joppa 156

iNDEX

SPINACH
history of 49
Alexandria Meat Loaf (Ham Roquefort) 157
Ham and Spinach Casserole 158
Miriam's Spinach Salad 63
Spinach Bacon Salad 61
Spinach in Cheese Sauce 57
Vegetables Carmel (Spinach and Green Onions) 60

SQUAB JERUSALEM 145

SQUASH
history of 48
Squash Fritters 60
Squash and Onions Jonah 64
Squash Pancakes 63
Stuffed Squash Elisha 67

SQUID
Stuffed Sicilian Squid 123

STOCK
Basic Beef 22
Basic Chicken 23

STUFFINGS
Apricot Date Stuffing 173
Bread and Shallot Stuffing 178
Shiloh Stuffing (Watercress) 179
Grape Stuffing 135
Lamb Stuffing 142
Oyster Stuffing 120
Watercress and Radish Stuffing 119
Wheat Pilaf Stuffing 134

SUMMER SAVORY
history and gardening 198

SWEET MARJORAM
history and gardening 198

SWEETBREADS
Baked Sweetbreads 175

TEAS, HERB 189

THYME
history and gardening 199

TONGUE
Potted Tongue 4
Tongues Corinth 174

TROUT
Grilled Jordan Trout 121

VEAL
history of 161
Cold Rolled Stuffed Breast of Veal 167
Fresh Minted Grilled Patties 169
Fricassee of Veal Medeba 170
Veal Mariamne with Groats Herod 166
Veal and Pork Bake 168
Veal Ring 169

VENISON
history of 149
Esau's Rotisserie Venison 153
Venison Stew 154

WALNUTS
history of 30

WATERCRESS
history of 48
Cream of Watercress Dothan 14
Kedish Summer Soup 16
Shiloh Stuffing 179
Spring Soup 15

Watercress and Radish Stuffing
119
Watercress Spread 2

WATERMELON
history of 28
Minted Melons 33
Shrimp in Melon 127
Watermelon Jam 42

WHEAT
Abram's Supper (Wheat and Bacon) 94
Ezekiel's Many-floured Bread 81
Spiced Bread Galatia 83

WHITEFISH
Baked Whitefish of Malta 118

WORMWOOD
history and gardening 199

YOGURT
Persian Cucumber and Yogurt Soup 15
Riblah Cheese 99
Wanderer's Joy (Yogurt Drink) 189
Yogurt 98
Yogurt Cake 102
Yogurt Cheese with Nuts 114